Mainline or Methodist?

Rediscovering Our Evangelistic Mission

SCOTT KISKER

DISCIPLESHIP RESOURCES

P.O. BOX 340003 • NASHVILLE, TN 37203-0003
www.discipleshipresources.org

Cover design by Shawn Lancaster

Interior design by PerfectType, Nashville, TN

ISBN 978-0-88177-541-9

Library of Congress Catalog in Publication Data on File

Contents

Foreword

As part of the baby-boom generation and a life-long member of the United Methodist Church, I have had the odd experience of spending my whole life in a church with an identity crisis. One of the questions people have always asked is, "What do United Methodist believe?" By this question, they did not merely want to learn about our doctrines, but also about our practices and our ethos. That was not an easy question for people in my generation. Of course, we knew that our church had a unique history. The stories of John Wesley preaching in the fields of Great Britain and Francis Asbury riding the circuits on the American frontier were colorful and appealed to those of us with a tinge of rebellion against the establishment. Yet, those stories were about a movement that existed a long time ago. Our church had a right to claim that history and to tell those stories, but they did not seem relevant to our identity today. The usual answer we would give to the question was that the United Methodist Church is a mainline Protestant denomination that is very similar to other mainline Protestant denominations except that we have a different form of church government and way of assigning pastors to congregations.

It is obvious to any observer that our church has changed considerably since its beginning. Change is to be expected since every living organism changes or dies. In a healthy organism, change over time does not destroy its identity. The problem with the United Methodist Church is that it seems to have lost its identity through all of its changes over the years. In other words, our church seems to have undergone mutations that disturbed the identity it possessed at its birth.

Consider all of the mutations through which the United Methodist Church has passed. Missionaries sent by John Wesley or Methodists who immigrated brought Methodism to America. These official and unofficial missionaries began to replicate in America the Methodist movement of Great Britain. Within the Episcopal Church and alongside it, there emerged Methodist societies composed of classes whose members sought to live the Christian life according to the General Rules. After the Methodist Episcopal Church was founded in 1784, Methodists embraced the new measures of evangelism that arose in the Second Great Awakening. An evangelical renewal movement established as a church mutated into an ecclesiastical institution of revivalism. A century later, the church went through another mutation as the theology and institutional forms of Protestant Liberalism quickly gained dominance. The focus of the church shifted from evangelism to nurture and from particular evangelical experience to general religious experience and ethics. Throughout all these mutations, the church did have success in gaining members and influence. No doubt, the success came in part from identifying closely with trends in American culture. Ironically, the moment that the church began to be proud of its achievements in American society and to call itself a mainline Protestant church was when it began its precipitous decline. The culture with which we had learned to identify had transformed rapidly into something very pluralistic and diverse, and it left on the sideline we who had been mainline.

The question for United Methodists today is, "Where do we go from here?" The answer to that question depends on whether our church will locate its identity in its relationship to the culture or in its origins as a movement of the Holy Spirit in history. To many of us, the answer is clear: the purpose of the United Methodist Church should be to embody the distinctive Wesleyan tradition of the apostolic and universal Christian faith. While we are not the only embodiment of this tradition everywhere, we do have primary responsibility to be a steward of this tradition in strategic locations. Our size and global reach give us opportunities other Wesleyan churches may have not. As our membership increases outside America, we shall find it easier to regain perspective on our church's relationship to American culture and begin to see ourselves as the embodiment of Wesleyan tradition around the world in diverse national and cultural settings.

I hope that my generation will be the last generation of United Methodists that has to endure the identity crisis of our church. Voices of new generations, like that of Dr. Scott Kisker, are calling us to appropriate the distinctive Wesleyan tradition for a new day. Claiming our identity as the embodiment of the Wesleyan tradition will not only solve our church's identity crisis, but also enable us to fulfill the mission of the body of Christ to be the means by which people hear the gospel, live holy lives, and witness to God's power to transform the world.

Tim W. Whitaker
Florida Area Resident Bishop
The United Methodist Church

Chapter One

The Mainline and Methodism

I turned forty this past year. I am a year older than the United Methodist Church. During my sabbatical, I began to experience all sorts of strange health problems that appeared to be unrelated. Basically, I thought this is what happens when you turn forty. I was treating all the different symptoms on my own until my wife and a friend convinced me I needed to see someone who is an actual doctor of *medicine*. It turned out all of these different symptoms were related, or related to the random way I was treating them. I have an auto-immune deficiency. There is something systemically wrong with me.

The point is I needed someone to tell me what I was going through was not normal. Then I needed a diagnosis.

Without a correct diagnosis, I would have continued mistreating symptoms and ultimately doing damage to myself without getting at the root cause.

Brothers and sisters, United Methodism, at forty, is systemically sick.

The Decline of Methodism

After a statement like that most United Methodists will assume that my main concern is the numerical shrinkage that has befallen the denomination since the 1960s. We expect the usual litany. At the time the United Methodist church was cobbled together from the Methodist Church and Evangelical United Brethren, we were the largest Protestant denomination in America with ten million members. We were the most representative religion in the U.S. ethnically and economically. Since that time, while the population as a whole has continued to increase, the United Methodist Church has shrunk by twenty percent in this country, and become less representative.

Depending on one's ecclesiastical politics and the spin one wants to put on the story behind these statistics, this decline since the 1960s is either a sign of greater faithfulness to the gospel or the abandonment of it.

In one telling of our story since mid-twentieth century, Methodism took a stand for civil rights, finally aligning itself with the message of liberation so clear in the teachings of our Lord. Mainstream culture then began to reject the radical aspects of the gospel just as it had rejected God's anointed two thousand years before. The so-called decline is simply the body of Christ living out the story of the crucifixion, bearing witness to the truth without concern for its own self-interest.

In another telling of the story, the 1960s saw the triumph of liberalism in the denominational structure. Methodism allowed the intellectual trends of the American academy and cultural elites to erode the truths of the gospel. By not emphasizing the uniqueness and universal Lordship of Jesus Christ, the necessity of Christ's death for the forgiveness of sins, the new birth, and the power of the Holy Spirit to live a new, holy life, Methodism lost its message. The church ceased to be part of God's work to transform people's lives, stopped converting people, and thus began to shrink.

One can argue both of these tales from the "facts" of history. It is true that the prophetic stance for civil rights was unpopular in large parts of society and our denomination. It is also true that the structure of the newly formed United Methodist Church marginalized evangelism. The various spins fit neatly into the liberal/conservative categories in which mainstream Americans have become accustomed to thinking.

However, any analysis of United Methodism's problems that focuses on the post-1960s period is in my mind misguided, not least because the sides of the conversation are predetermined and it is thus likely to be fruitless. This is why, as a denomination, we find ourselves

11

without a common story and facing (as we seem to every four years at General Conference) the prospect of schism.

It is also wrong for us to focus on the changes in the larger society. Methodism's decline is not society's fault. The problems facing Methodism are not external to us. Society has indeed changed dramatically since WWII. Society also changed dramatically in the eighteenth and nineteenth centuries, and yet Methodism thrived. Furthermore, Christian traditions (like Pentecostalism) rooted in Methodism and, at least on the surface, appear much less likely to interact with modern or post-modern worldviews than we mainliners, have seen nearly exponential growth in the twentieth and the beginning of the twenty-first centuries.

It is my contention that by focusing on the post-1960s or on the surrounding culture, we are misdiagnosing the nature of Methodism's decline and the reason for that decline. While the numbers are relevant, focusing on statistics is also misleading. As I observe the history of Methodism in this country, I would argue that the decline of Methodism began decades before the denomination experienced any numerical losses. Both the resistance to civil rights and the marginalization of evangelism were symptoms of the same disease—one that had gone on for years undiagnosed. Even our complaints about a "changed society" are a clue to what is wrong. Methodism has had an unholy alliance with that larger society.

"Mainline" Religion

For us in so-called mainline Methodism, our "mainline" identity is killing us and we must surgically remove if we are ever to regain our health. When we became "mainline," we stopped actually being Methodist in all but name. Real Methodism declined within our so-called "Methodist" churches well before people stopped wanting to join them. Real Methodism declined because we replaced those peculiarities that made us Methodist with a bland, acceptable, almost civil religion, barely distinguishable from other traditions also now known as "mainline." Like the Israelites under the judges, we wanted to be like the other nations. We no longer wanted to be an odd, somewhat disreputable people. And we have begun to reap the consequences.

If Methodists are to begin our recovery, we must do so, first, by recognizing the fiction that is "mainline." There is no such thing as a "mainline" church. No one has ever joined one. No one has ever promised to uphold the "Mainline Church" with prayers, presence, gifts, and service. When we take membership vows, we do so as Methodists, Presbyterians, Episcopalians or Lutherans, denominations that have very different Christian traditions. These traditions differ theologically, liturgically, and organization. Is it not strange that, as different as they are, they have been lumped together, or have lumped themselves together, under a pseudo-tradition called "mainline?" And all are in crisis.

The earliest printed reference to "mainline churches" according to the Oxford English Dictionary is April 15, 1972 in the *Times*, right around the time United Methodism came into existence as a denomination. The word appears in an article in which some young people said, "The mainline churches have sold out to the establishment." That is exactly the point.

I went to college just outside Philadelphia. There the term "mainline" has a slightly older usage. It refers to a train line that runs through the most elite suburbs of that city—where the establishment live. Mainline protestantism is the religion of the establishment. Not coincidentally, most of the mainline churches, which William Hutchinson has referred to as the "seven sisters of American Protestantism," (another reference to an elite establishment) are historically connected to the European State Churches.

What makes mainline churches "mainline" is that they identify with the establishment, either liberal or conservative, depending on where they are located. To paraphrase Jim Logan, my predecessor in the chair of Evangelism at Wesley Theological Seminary in Washington DC, mainline denominations are like what he calls pillar congregations, "They bless the values of the larger society, and see very little difference between cultivating good citizens and cultivating Christians."

Look at the last two U.S. presidential administrations. The first families have both had prominent United Methodists—Hillary Rodham Clinton, and George W.

Bush. Too many United Methodists think this is a badge of honor. We fail to ask, "What makes these two people Methodist? What do they share theologically? What do they share in their understanding of the kingdom of God in society? Perhaps a creative theologian could come up with something, but I suspect what the two of them share most in common is that they were raised in upper-middle class American homes among comfortable society. United Methodism simply baptized the versions of establishment religion as they existed in Northern Illinois and Texas. The phenomenon of these two political leaders sharing a denomination is possible only because United Methodism has become simply a reflection of the middle and upper middle class world around it.

Methodism and the "Mainline"

Ironically, Methodism didn't start out as part of this club. The Wesleys and the movement they oversaw were an embarrassment to the Anglican communion and mainline society. When we came to the American continent, people regarded Methodists as low class at best and dangerous at worst. The line in the movie *A River Runs Through It* where a 1920s Presbyterian minister refers to Methodists contemptuously as "Baptists who can read" captures the sentiment quite accurately. Contrast the state of Methodism today with Bishop Francis Asbury's assessment in his valedictory address as bishop.

As to temporal power, what have we to do with that in this country? We are not senators, congressmen, or chaplains; neither do we hold any civil offices. We neither have, nor wish to have, anything to do with the government of the States, nor, as I conceive, do the States fear us. Our kingdom is not of this world. For near half a century we have never grasped at power. (*The Journal and Letters of Francis Asbury*, 3 vols., ed. Elmer T. Clark et al., [Nashville: Abingdon Press, 1958] 3:480, 5 August 1813.)

Even before the term "mainline" was coined, things had begun to change for us. Certainly by World War II, we Methodists had successfully achieved respectability and gained our membership card in the club of establishment religion. Moreover, it thrilled us because we had worked hard at getting in. Donald Dayton, one of my former professors, used to date Methodism's respectability much earlier. He used to say, "When Methodist Bishop Matthew Simpson performed Abraham Lincoln's funeral, the whole denomination breathed a sigh of relief." We could begin to relax. We had arrived. We had made it into the vestibule of the club of respectability and of influence. We were becoming part of the establishment.

Methodism in the late nineteenth and even more so in the early twentieth century was nearly obsessed with its own respectability. Our recently founded educational institutions had to be acceptable to the standards of the modern academy, no matter how far from the gospel those standards deviated. Our buildings had to compete with the best of civic architecture. Our music had to be of the highest cultural standards. We even began to assume we deserved to determine the shape of American society, not through conversion, a process of repentance and new birth, but through the political process and our own lobby, located in a fine white building across the street from the U.S. Capitol.

This did not happen without some fallout. Our growing comfort with the ways American mainstream culture saw the splitting off of smaller denominations made up of more radical and more working-class segments of the denomination. One can read as part of this dynamic the history of the formation of the African Methodist Episcopal Church and the African Methodist Episcopal Church, Zion. Certainly, the establishment of the Free Methodist Church, the Wesleyan Methodist Church, and the Nazarene Church exemplify it.

Those lost members were, however, soon replaced. The middle class was expanding. The denomination continued to grow numerically, but not much beyond the rate of population growth and not always that much. Yet, we were the largest denomination in America. Methodists began to think of ourselves as defining religiously what it means to be American. In 1890s, the General Conference decided to establish an educational institution in the nation's capital, partly, no doubt, to counterbalance The Catholic University (founded by Pope Leo XIII in 1887). Ours would be called, not "The Methodist University," but The American University.

By the 1950s, we were taking part in respectable ecumenical conversations with the other mainline and state churches throughout the world. We no longer viewed our founder as an evangelist, a man caught up in a movement of the Holy Spirit. He became a "theologian," if only a "folk" one. Those years proved to be mainline Methodism's high point in terms of raw numbers and influence. By then, the Methodist Church had shed most of its idiosyncrasies and could carry the banner of family, freedom, and a nondescript establishment American Christianity.

The 1960s and the civil rights movements revealed deep fissures within American culture. By the 1970s, when the term "mainline" was coming into common usage, the handwriting was already on the wall. What happened among all "mainline" churches in the following decades was a desperate attempt to downplay anything distinctively different from what they perceived to be American mainstream culture, and to emphasize an ever-shrinking area of consensus. This, we believed, would both hold on to members and fulfill our self-designated responsibility to hold together American society. Now it seems, the only thing mainline churches stand for is diversity and inclusion. "Open hearts, open doors, open minds."

This brings us to Methodism's current confusion about both mission and evangelism. Because we assume ourselves part of the establishment, in the minds of most United Methodists words like "mission" and "evangelism" are inevitably about what *we* are able to do. In mission, we serve those less fortunate than we are. We make a difference in the world for Jesus. We "build the kingdom of God." And if we use the word "evangelism" at all, we think it means we do good marketing for our congregations. We recruit people into the club.

The assumption is that if we get our acts together, if we get our politics right, if we use the right business models, if we hire the right PR firm, if we do the right kind of motivation, *we* will solve our numbers problems. Mission becomes an exercise in of *noblesse oblige* or of political coercion (however benevolent) in the name of God's will for society. Evangelism gets reduced to technique, a "how to" cookbook to achieve a given result. The focus is on us. It assumes *we* (privileged establishment people) have it in us to do what is expected of us. We don't really need grace. It is, at root, heretical. Contemporary mainline Methodism has become Pelagian.

The Double Conversion of John Wesley

Despite what I see as our gradual abandonment over the last century or so of what made us alive, I do believe Methodism could revive even within the United Methodist Church. That is the reason for this book. But for this to happen, it will require United Methodists to humble ourselves. And we who claim John Wesley as our founder are fortunate. We already have a model for what this might look like.

John Wesley was born into respectability. Now I know that many of us have heard stories of the Wesley family's financial difficulties—John's father being thrown into jail for debt and his mother coming before a judge and saying that though she did not want for bread, she had to expend much energy to get it. However, if one visits the house built by John's father in Epworth, with its grand Queen Anne staircase and more windows than the family could afford to pay the window taxes on, one realizes that any difficulties the Wesley family had came more from mismanagement than from lack of resources.

Despite whatever suffering the family endured, whatever financial hurdles, all the sons of the Wesley family were educated in the elite preparatory boarding schools of Charterhouse and Westminster. All attended Oxford University. By the standards of their own day—or even our own—they were very privileged. They had a position in society. They were part of the establishment.

On May 24, 1738, John Wesley, this privileged young clergyman, this Oxford don, this world traveler, went very unwillingly to a society meeting in Aldersgate Street. Many of you probably know the story from there. Someone was reading from Luther's Preface to the Epistle to the Romans and John had his heart "warmed." He experienced the forgiving love of God as he had not experienced it before. He found himself trusting the gospel so deeply that he was sure (received an assurance) that God had forgiven him personally and loved him personally.

As important as that moment was in John's life, we must realized that any number of privileged people in the eighteenth century experienced that kind of conversion. What created the movement known as Methodism was not that moment in a meeting on Aldersgate Street, but something that happened a year later. On Saturday, March 31, 1739, John Wesley made his first visit to Bristol. George Whitfield, who had been a student with Charles at Oxford and a member of the Wesleys' Oxford Holy Club, invited him. Whitfield wanted Wesley to take over the religious work of taking the gospel *outside* the buildings of the established church, to the common people, on their turf.

On April 1, Wesley and Whitfield went to the bowling green, two blocks from where Wesley would later build the first Methodist meeting room. There, Whitfield preached outside. Later that day, John followed Whitfield out to Hanham Mount, a natural, open-air preaching arena. People knew that Whitfield was leaving Bristol the following day for a preaching tour of America. Crowds gathered to hear this squint-eyed preacher. Wesley looked out at a sea of poor miners with their faces blackened by coal dust. This was not Wesley's crowd. It was all so unseemly. Could it be Christian?

That evening Wesley went to a religious society meeting, which met on Nicholas Street in Bristol. He had been asked to teach on the Sermon on the Mount. He recorded in his *Journal*, "One pretty remarkable precedent of field preaching."

The following day, Wesley was left alone in Bristol. Whitfield was gone. But Whitfield had left him a challenge. He had made an appointment for Wesley to preach in the Brickyard, an industrial part of the city where the bricks were being made for the city's first sewer. Wesley recorded:

> At four in the afternoon, I submitted to be more vile, and proclaimed in the highways the glad tidings of salvation . . . The Scripture on which I spoke was this . . . "The spirit of the Lord is upon me, because he hath anointed me to preach the gospel to the poor. He hath sent to heal the broken hearted; to preach deliverance to the captives and recovery of sight to the blind; to set at liberty them that are bruised, to proclaim the acceptable year of the Lord." (*Journal*, April 1, 1739, *The Works of John Wesley*, [Jackson], vol. 1.)

More vile. If Wesley had sought only to reach out with the good news of the kingdom to those in his social circle, those to whom he could easily relate, there would have been no religious awakening. Instead, Wesley's first sermon in the open air echoed Jesus' own anointing, to preach good news to the poor. The text Wesley chose for this sermon is the same text with which Jesus began his ministry in the synagogue in Nazareth. It comes from Isaiah 61, the vision of the prophet for the Jubilee year. It is a vision of the End Times beginning now in the lives of simple humble people.

We United Methodists have become a privileged lot.

We are educated well beyond the majority in our society. We pay our clergy, as distinctly mainline, beyond the majority in our society. If we are to recover Methodism, freed from its addiction to the American mainstream, it will require the kind of conversion Wesley experienced that day in Bristol. It is a conversion to God and neighbor because we are witnesses to God's ultimate kingdom of the new creation. For such a recovery, we must humble ourselves before almighty God, trust in the sacrifice and resurrection of Jesus Christ, and expect a blessing through a miraculous anointing by the Holy Spirit. Following that we must take some risky, perhaps uncomfortable steps. We must allow a vision, a message, and a discipline to capture us, one that is quite at odds with our present age, its establishment, and its principalities and powers.

Conclusion: Recovering Methodism

I hope the following chapters will be both convicting and encouraging. In them, I will describe what I believe a recovery of healthy, living Methodism within United Methodism might look like. To do this, I will point out those parts of our identity I believe we need to reappropriate as we resist the urge to become "like other nations." Another historian might come up with other markers for what it means to be Methodist. Those I am presenting come from my reading of Methodist history and theology as I observe the current state of our church. My contention is that our traditional under-standing of what God desires for the world, what it means for individuals to be saved, and the practices that flow from these understandings, are peculiar and inter-connected. These theological and practical assertions set us apart and give our tradition its reason for existence within the larger Church. In theological terms, our eschatology defines our soteriology, which determines our methodology.

In the following chapter, I will look at how Methodism has understood the purpose of it all—God's desire for creation. Chapter three will look at how we have understood what it looks like for individuals to par-ticipate in the new creation, to be part of God's kingdom on earth. In Chapter four, I will examine the practices Methodism developed as an organization. These prac-tices were not arbitrary. They functioned as means of grace, to work with God in what God is doing in the world and in the lives of people bringing them into con-tact with the new creation and God's kingdom. Chapter five will look at how Methodists have discerned God's will and direction for their time, through holy conferenc-ing. Finally, chapter six will give some suggestions for how a community (even a United Methodist one) might reform itself along Methodist lines.

Would this reform reduce our falling numbers? I don't know and, to a large degree, I don't care. I do think it would put the people who call themselves Methodists at the forefront of God's saving work in the world again.

We would be Methodists in more than name. And we would do what we, by a series of strange providences in the eighteenth century, were established to do.

Chapter Two

A Vision

When I first went to college, I planned to become a medical missionary. I knew I wanted to serve God and my father was a medical professor, so it seemed like a fit. My sophomore year, I decided medical school was not in the cards. I dropped chemistry and enrolled in a course in American Intellectual History. I waited the two weeks until the add/drop period was over and called my dad to let him know. His reaction, it turned out, in no way deserved the anxiety with which I had invested it. Plus, I found that I loved my history course in ways that I had never loved biology or chemistry. I enrolled in more history courses the next semester, and before the year was out declared myself a history major.

That spring my father came to Philadelphia for a conference and took several of my friends and me out to dinner. During the course of that one meal, he must have asked the same question five times. "So . . . what do you do with a history major?" Each time he asked, I sort of hemmed and hawed, and gave some lame answer, which is why ten minutes later he had to ask again. That question, "So . . . what do you do with a history major?" became a running joke between those friends and me for the remainder of our years in college. It still comes up occasionally some twenty years later.

My father wanted to know what my goal was. What was all this study (and, let's be honest, money) leading to? What did I want to do with the life God had given me? The reason he had to keep asking was that I didn't have a clue. I had no sense of the purpose of my education. I was floating along, without a calling, without a vision. Only years later did I begin to discern God's calling, ironically that revelation was also connected with my father's annoying pragmatic questions.

John Wesley's Vision

What drove John Wesley and the early Methodists to humiliate themselves for the sake of the gospel? What gave John Wesley the courage to risk looking like a fool in the eyes of other Oxford dons? What made early American circuit riders destroy their health and often sacrifice their lives for little or no pay? It was not for a career, not even a particularly good example of "church," neither Church of England nor Methodist Episcopal. It was for something much bigger, much more important than anything this world has to offer, and yet something not "otherworldly."

John Wesley as an undergraduate was also a bit unfocused. He was a good student, but did not distinguish himself from his fellow students in piety or virtue. Upon graduation, however, he decided to enter the family business to become a priest in the Church of England. Recounting the highlights of his spiritual journey, John Wesley wrote in his *Journal*:

> When I was about twenty-two, my father pressed me to enter into holy orders. At the same time, the providence of God directing me to Kempis' *Christian Pattern* [*The Imitation of Christ*], I began to see that true religion was seated in the heart, and that God's law extended to all our thoughts as well as words and actions . . . and meeting likewise with a religious friend, which I had never had till now, I began to alter the whole form of my conversation and to set in earnest upon a new life . . . I began to aim at and pray for *inward holiness*. (*Journal*, from February 1, 1738-August 12, 1738, *Works*, [Jackson], vol. 1.)

Partly because of his father's pressing, John had been awakened to something beyond the everyday concerns of life, even beyond his father's concerns for his career. As he read the works of the early Church Fathers, and English devotional works his mother recommended, a particular vision of the Christian life and of the Church captured John—one he carried for the rest of his life. It was a vision of simplicity, of holiness. It was a vision of something beyond this world, being made tangible in this world—of human life that looked very different from everyday humanity.

I have often said to my students, if you catch John Wesley's vision, the rest of his theology and methodology falls into place.

This vision is the possibility of present salvation from the tyranny of sin—from the dominion of the devil. It is a vision of a life lived under the authority of God, who brings "liberty to the captives" (Is 61:1). It is St. Peter's vision of a "royal priesthood, a holy nation, God's own people" (1 Pet 2:9), living in accord with God's will, as a visible testimony to resurrection power. The "beauty of holiness" (1 Chr 16:29) had seduced Wesley long before his Aldersgate experience. That pursuit became his calling.

It Is All About Holiness

Wesley knew God wanted something greater of him, of us, of God's church. But, for Wesley, holiness was not something added to what we are now. It meant the restoration of what we were created to be—the restoration of the image of God.

Eight years before his experience of having his heart warmed, Wesley preached a sermon on "The Image of

God." God's intention in creation, he said, was that humanity be "what God is, Love." Adam, before his rejection of God's authority, is the model for what God intends for humanity. According to Wesley, "Love filled the whole expansion of his soul; it possessed him without rival." As he later articulated it, this vision of holiness was the kingdom of God within us. In his sermon "Sermon on the Mount, VI," he wrote:

> In order that the name of God might be hallowed, we pray that his kingdom, the kingdom of Christ, may come This kingdom then comes to a particular person, when he "repents and believes the gospel; when he is taught of God, not only to know himself, but to know Jesus Christ and him crucified. As "this is life eternal, to know the only true God, and Jesus Christ whom he hath sent;" so it is the kingdom of God begun below, set up in the believer's heart; "the Lord God Omnipotent" then "reigneth," when he is known through Christ Jesus. He taketh unto himself his mighty power, that he may subdue all things unto himself.

For Wesley, the Lordship of Christ, the kingdom of God, God's will being done on earth as it is in heaven, is the reason Jesus came. Jesus' "humbled himself, and became obedient to the point of death—even death on a cross" (Phil 2:8) to restore us to the obedience of love— to make us into that holy priesthood, ministering to creation like Adam and Eve in the Garden. God sent Jesus to create a people set apart, sanctified, saints. God's love was incarnate that we might become God's love incarnate. The Law of Love was fulfilled in Christ. And by the Holy Spirit God's law of love can also fill us.

RECEIVED BY GRACE THROUGH FAITH

The problem was that Wesley could not make himself love, could not will himself to obey. He tried, through disciplined holy clubs, through missionary service, even by preaching to others what he had not yet experienced himself. But he could not achieve sainthood.

Aldersgate was important because it was the first indication in Wesley's own life that what he had read about in the Scriptures, in the Church Fathers, in works of practical divinity, and heard testified to by others, was real. He experienced himself, a degree of God's assurance, of righteousness, and of peace. "An assurance was *given* me," he wrote in his *Journal*, "that [God] had taken away my sins, even mine, and saved me from the law of sin and death." (*Journal* May 24, 1738, *Works*, [Jackson], vol.)

John Wesley learned at that meeting in Aldersgate Street that holiness, saintliness, victory over sin, resurrection, the kingdom of God, is a gift. We can do nothing to deserve it. We cannot achieve it. That does not mean we humans are completely passive. We can earnestly seek it; indeed we must "seek first the kingdom" (Mt 6:33). But most importantly, we can and must receive it by faith. Only then will there be a "new creation" (2 Co 5:17). As his brother Charles Wesley described it, this experience was a real foretaste of the new creation, an "antepast of heaven."

PERFECTED IN LOVE

Shortly after his heartwarming experience, John continued in his *Journal*:

> After my return home, I was much buffeted with temptations, but cried out, and they fled away. They returned again and again. I as often lifted up my eyes, and he "sent me help from his holy place" and herein I found the difference between this and my former state chiefly consisted. I was striving, yea, fighting with all my might under the law, as well as under grace. But then I was sometimes, if not often, conquered; now, I was always conqueror. (*Journal* May 24, 1738, *Works*, [Jackson], vol. 1.)

This always conquering did not last very long. Only five days later John confessed in his journal that he did "grieve the Holy Spirit." He was also not sure he had experienced the requisite joy he thought should be associated with his new birth, though he did have peace. Throughout his ministry, Wesley acknowledged that he, at any given moment, was more or less experiencing what he preached. He went through periods of doubt. But the knowledge that something beyond him was near to him, that heaven on earth was not simply something in the Bible, not simply something for Jesus, the apostles, the early church, not simply for others, but for him, and by extension, for everybody, transformed his ministry.

What he discovered not too long after Aldersgate was that the new birth was not the fullness of the kingdom here and now. But he did not give up on the vision of holiness he had seen in the Scriptures and the accounts of the Church Fathers. The new birth was not the fullest possible expression of holiness in this life. It was a birth. It was not the goal of Christianity, it was the doorway to it, and there was a lot of house left to explore. Though born again, Wesley was not yet perfected in love, not entirely sanctified, not a complete saint.

This was the logic behind Wesley's understanding of Christian perfection. Perfection, completeness, is the greatest manifestation of the love of God filling us that is possible in this life. We can be perfected in love, not because we work hard enough at it, but because our hope is only in God's grace. As Wesley assures us in his sermon "The Scripture Way of Salvation," we may be made perfect in love because "God hath promised it in the Holy Scripture. . . . What God hath promised he is able to perform. . . . [and] He is willing and able to do it now." ."("Scripture Way of Salvation" *Works* [Jackson], vol 6.)

Because God is all-powerful, because God desires God's creatures to be filled with God's love, we can be saved to the uttermost here and now. That is Wesley's understanding of perfection. And because this change is possible in us here and now, all sorts of changes are possible here and now.

SPREADING AND REFORMING

This vision of holiness was behind the mission of Methodism as articulated by those societies in Wesley's connection. In The Large Minutes the question was asked, "What may we reasonably believe to be God's design in raising up the preachers called Methodist?" The answer was: "to reform the nation, particularly the Church; and to spread scriptural holiness over the land." (*Wesley, Works* [Jackson], vol. 8.)

The kingdom of God is not only present to individuals, it is present to "the nation, and especially to the Church." As Wesley looked at history and at the struggles of his own age, he did so through the eyes of faith. He believed in the final triumph of love in the world. Christ would come in final victory. He believed that God made promises and fulfilled those promises in history. He believed the gospel would spread to the ends of the earth. And he believed God, the Holy Spirit, was active now in history to bring about God's promises.

In his sermon on "The Signs of the Times" Wesley wrote:

> We allow, indeed, that in every age of the Church, "the kingdom of God came not with observation;" not with splendour and pomp, or with any of those outward circumstances which usually attend the kingdoms of this world. We allow this "kingdom of God is within us;" and that consequently, when it begins either in an individual or in a nation, it "is like a grain of mustard seed," which

at first "is the least of all seeds," but nevertheless, gradually increases, till "it becomes a great tree." Or, to use the other comparison of our Lord, it is like "a little leaven, which a woman took and hid in three measures of meal, till the whole was leavened." ("The Signs of the Times," *Works*, [Jackson], vol. 6.)

The gospel, embodied by a people possessed by it, can change things. A number of years ago David Lowes Watson wrote an article titled "Prophetic Evangelism: The Good News of Global Grace." In that article, he expanded the idea of conversion to the systems of power in this world. They can be chastened through the Church's witness to holiness. They may be forgiven and receive new life by grace through faith. "Communities, cities, nation, conglomerates," he wrote, "must not only be analyzed as sinful, but must be called to repentance, and can *be expected to repent.*" (David Lowes Watson, Prophetic Evangelism: The Good News of Global Grace," *Wesleyan Spirituality Today* [Nashville: UM Publishing House, 1985], 222.) And all this is God's doing.

Lest we think this is too great a stretch, we need only remind ourselves of John Wesley's last letter was to William Wilberforce, the parliamentarian who eventually succeeded in abolishing the slave trade in the British Empire. Wesley wrote:

> Unless the divine power has raised you up to be as Athanasius, *contra mundum,* [St. Athanasius against the world], I see not how you can go through your glorious enterprise in opposing that

execrable villainy, which is the scandal of religion, of England, and of human nature. Unless God has raised you up for this very thing, you will be worn out by the opposition of men and devils. But if God be for you, who can be against you? Are all of them together stronger than God? O "be not weary of well-doing." Go on, in the name of God and in the power of his might, till even American slavery, the vilest that ever saw the sun, shall vanish away before it. (Wesley, "Letter to William Wilberforce," 27 February 1791, *Works* [Jackson], vol. 13.)

God was at work and God is at work. God's kingdom was at hand and God's kingdom is at hand. If we, or anyone else, repents and believes, we may enter into it. The kingdom is God's intention for human beings in relation to God and our neighbor, and "all creation waits in eager expectation" (Rom 8:19) for us to enter it.

We, in our strength, cannot change the world. We, a motley group of freed slaves, are too weak to come against the powerful forces that occupy the land. But God can, and whenever we are weak, God is strong.

On Wesley's deathbed he is reported to have said, "And best of all, God is with us." Wesley's deathbed statement was not arrogant boasting but a realization that God is all in all. This Methodist movement, which he oversaw, existed only because of what God had done. Wesley believed it was God's providence, power, and presence that had brought it about and changed so much.

The Vision in the American Context

This vision of the present reality of the kingdom of God, experientially available to all today, carried over into Methodism as it was expressed on this side of the Atlantic but it rather quickly got confused with the vision of America. Russell Richey has documented how early American Methodists committed themselves, at least rhetorically, to the reign of God, not on the new nation.

Of course, they were aware of their new context for ministry. They had endured persecution during the revolution for their connections to Wesley and the Church of England. They were the first denomination to organize themselves nationally. However, their primary allegiance was not to a new nation but to God's kingdom, which was for them a present, and a future, reality. They saw America as an opportunity, an opening for the gospel that had been so hindered in Europe by privileged churches entangled in and compromised by their involvement with the State.

In his letter to the American preachers, at the time of the formation of the American church, Wesley wrote, "They are now at liberty to follow the scriptures and the primitive church. And we judge it best that they should stand fast in that liberty wherewith God has so strangely made them free."

Asbury wrote in 1789, "The number of candidates for the ministry are many; from which circumstance I am led to think the Lord is about greatly to enlarge the borders of Zion." Asbury's wrote in 1802:

> My general experience is close communion
> with God, holy fellowship with the Father and his
> Son Jesus Christ, a will resigned, frequent addresses
> to a throne of grace, a constant serious care for the
> prosperity of Zion, forethought in the arrangements
> and appointments of the preachers, a soul drawn
> out in ardent prayer for the universal Church and
> the complete triumph of Christ over the whole
> earth. (*Journal and Letters of Francis Asbury*, 3:372, 28
> December 1802.)

"Zion" was a Methodist's true country. It was a term
that reoccurred throughout the journals of Methodist
itinerant preachers.

Methodists had a mission and a vision that was
beyond the Nation. In adapting the mission which
Wesley had articulated for the Methodists in England,
William McKendree said in his 1816 episcopal address,
"Beloved Brethren, We believe God's design in raising up
the preachers called Methodists in America, was to
reform the continent by spreading scriptural holiness
over these lands." (Robert Paine, *Life and Times of
William McKendree*, 2 vols. [Nashville: MECS Pub. Hse.]
1:347-8.) American Methodists would reform, not just
the Nation, but also the continent by spreading scriptural holiness over many lands.

Historians often refer to the period of American religious history between the Revolution and the Civil War
as the Second Great Awakening. Those who were caught

up in the revivals knew that they were part of a work of God in their midst. God's reign had broken and they could reasonably expect things outside of the "natural order." People could be transformed. Healings could take place. Social injustices could be abolished. Scriptural holiness could spread across the land. God could reign.

A 1792 quarterly meeting described by the itinerant preacher, Ezekiel Cooper, captures the sense. (Those of you who are United Methodist and have been to a quarterly meeting, or any United Methodist meetings, will probably note some differences from your usual experience. Cooper wrote:

> Saturday, February 18, 1792. We went on the quarterly meeting. The house was crowded. We had a tolerable time.
>
> Sunday, 19. In love-feast the Lord was previous, but in the time of preaching he opended the windows of heaven and poured down blessings upon us. Sinners were struck as with hammer and fire, or like as if thunder flashes had smitten them. A general cry began, so that I was forced to stop preaching. I stood upon the stand and looked on, and saw them in every part of the congregation with streaming eyes, and groaning for mercy, while others were shouting praises to God for delivering grace. Numbers were converted—the season was truly glorious and very refreshing to God's dear people. The meeting never broke up till about sundown. (George A. Phoebus, *Beams of Light on*

A Vision

Early Methodism in America [New York: Phillips and
Hunt, 1887], 142.)

This sense of the present living power of the Spirit
drove Methodism.

The establishment of a country with freedom of religion, and the fruit of these revivals (mass conversions,
and reform movements) led people to believe God was
fulfilling prophecy through the events of their day. And
God was. However, early Methodism's expression of the
coming kingdom does not fit comfortably within contemporary categories of liberal and conservative, or of
End Times speculation.

These early revivalists also had a strong sense of
God's impending judgment when evil would be finally
defeated and God's will would be done on earth as it is
in heaven. They also saw that judgment and transformation happening miraculously, here and now.

The journal of the first bishop of the Evangelical
Association, a branch of German Speaking Methodists,
who often held joint camp meetings with Methodist
Episcopalians, provides an example. He wrote in
September 1823 about one such event:

> There came a melting power from heaven upon
> the people and where the text refers to "terrible as
> an army with banners," I applied that to the coming
> of Jesus in Judgment. And he shall come with many
> thousand holy angels to judge the ungodly, and a
> destructive fire goes before him, ushering in a day
> that shall burn like a furnace. And then there was a

trembling and weeping among the people. One sister began to leap and shout. (John Seybert, *Journal of Bishop John Seybert*, trans. J.G. Eller [Ann Arbor: University Microfilms] Sunday, 19 January 1823.)

Now and Not Yet

Wesleyan Christians had a view of sanctification, which was both progressive and instantaneous. This view, in many ways, corresponded to the two aspects of their view of the coming kingdom of God.

On the one hand, sanctification was a gradual process which began when one was converted and culminated when one had "completed the race" at death. It was a divine human action/reaction whereby we "work out our salvation with fear and trembling." On the other hand, sanctification was a gift, an experience that one could and should expect to receive in an instant.

In the realm of society, God was fulfilling prophesy in preparation for Christ's second coming. This fulfillment was seen in the repentance and gradual improvement of societal structures (thus Democracy, temperance, and the anti-slavery movements) to be ready for the final harvest. This aspect of social sanctification, like individual sanctification, involved human effort working with the Holy Spirit. On the other hand, the full sanctification of creation would be realized in an instant, with the final judgment.

An Odd Society

This extremism made Methodists seem an odd, unsavory, even dangerous group to those for whom stability in society was a good thing. Methodist churches were called societies, and they were intended to represent a saving alternative to the destructive forces within the broader society.

An excerpt from Stith Mead's route to Methodism quoted by Russell Richey dramatizes this:

> Jan. 1790—Mr. Samuel Mead, a brother next youngest to me, who appears to be a sincere penitent for his sins, and myself traveled to the State of Georgia, to see our relations, whose god is in this world, with the rich and fashionable gay. I strove to encourage my brother, as I was a believer unto salvation, and he was only a seeker of religion. In Feb. We arrived in Georgia, and was received with much persecution from many of our relations, who soon raised a dancing party, when my brother was caught in the snare of Satan—I was much persuaded to stay and partake with them, but refused; having several miles to ride to Col. A. Gordon's, a brother-in-law, where I lived. My sisters often danced before me, others suggested I was deranged, and soon would be raving mad—but blessed by God, in the midst of all my temptations and trials, I find him to be a "friend that sticketh by me, nigher than a brother." I often took up my cross with a trembling hand, to pray in my father's family. .(Stith Mead, *A Short Account of the Experience and Labor of the Rev. Stith Mead*, Lynchburg, 1829, 47-8 quoted in Russell Richey, Early American Methodism [Indianapolis: Indiana University Press, 1991], 55.)

We might think Mead's portrayal of dancing as the snare of Satan a bit petty and moralistic. However, as Richey points out, this rejection of his family's social behavior is also a rejection of the genteel society to which he, by birth, belonged. Mead, like Wesley was not aspiring to higher social status. He was no longer primarily identifying with his own social class. Those who had access to "society"—like Mead—could be a part of a Methodist society, but not on their terms. They had to humble themselves, repent, and believe. Contemporary United Methodists' negative reactions to these restrictions may tell us more about ourselves and the society to which we are primarily committed.

Those who chose to participate in early American Methodism were disciplined according to a set of rules at odds with those of the surrounding culture. In its rhetoric and practice, early Methodism condemned what it called worldliness—where what determines our way of life are the economic, social, and political constructs of the present age. The written and unwritten rules of Methodism's societies, which prohibited dancing, gambling, and slave holding, were set over against the conduct of the slave-holding elites.

"Double-Minded and Unstable" (James 1:7)

Methodism in America did not maintain this sense of distinctiveness very long. Perhaps it is better to say, they had it and gave it up almost simultaneously.

Despite this sense of Zion, those early Methodists who moved most easily into the broader culture quickly found they had divided loyalties. These divisions became most evident as Methodism confronted issues of race and slavery.

The first group of Methodists in New York City included three recent immigrants, a slave, and a hired man. Small as it was, it included people of African and European descent, recent immigrants and native born citizens, slaves and freemen. Methodism began among the multi-ethnic poorer segments of society. They could easily identify with "the least of these."

The Christmas conference of 1784, which officially birth the Methodist Episcopal Church, decried slavery as "contrary to the Golden Law of God," and declared that Methodists were to have a year to begin emancipating their slaves, and five years in which to finish it. The alternatives were voluntary withdrawal or expulsion from the society.

In 1789 when the General Rules were first introduced into the *Discipline* of the Methodist Episcopal Church, they included a rule on slavery, prohibiting "the buying and selling the bodies and souls of men, women, and children with an intention to enslave them." Before six months were up, however, a long process of Phariseeism (seeing how far the wording of the Law could be pressed) and outright compromise had already begun. The compromises were made for the sake of unity (one could even say, inclusivity) but they ultimately shattered unity.

In 1790 the United States passed the Naturalization Law that made race an explicit legal category by limiting the right of naturalization to "free white person[s]." Such distinctions based on skin color increased as voting rights were extended beyond property owners. In the 1820s and 1830s, the right to vote was granted to all white males, but was taken away from some free blacks, who had been previously granted that right. "American" was increasingly defined as someone of European descent.

That same year, William McKendree, who would later become a bishop, described a quarterly meeting where segregation had already become the norm. "Brother Paup preached to the white congregation; I went into the grove with the Black people, and of a truth Jesus was there." (Robert Paine, *Life and Times of William McKendree*, 2 vols. [Nashville: MECS Pub Hse, 18740 I:127, 30 October 1790.) The kingdom was present among Methodists, but most powerfully among those to whom the promise of "America" was gradually being withdrawn.

As some Methodists divided their loyalties between Zion and America, the divisions of America became Methodism's divisions. When Methodists looked to the Nation as their source of hope, they took their eye off the promise of holiness and the present reality of a kingdom, which is in this world by the power of the Holy Spirit but not of this world.

Our experience of the Holy Spirit in our midst had empowered Methodists to form an alternative society. The experience of God's present but not fully present kingdom inspired our work in the social sphere. But our social location early on mitigated against any triumphalism, or the use of coercion to fulfill God's designs. Methodists did not have access to worldly power. When Euro-Methodists abandoned some of our brothers and sisters to accept a place at America's table, we were deceiving ourselves that we could use the power that went with the position to do good. We didn't notice we were being changed by that power. We became worldly, not holy.

Recovering a Vision of the End Now

Wesley knew that something that was beyond himself had gripped him. The rule of God had broken through with power. It had changed his understanding of God. It had changed his understanding of what was possible for God in his heart, in his actions, and in the world. John Wesley very consciously strived to be a man of reason. He was a careful thinker. He respected science. But he was also unabashedly committed to the supernatural.

As I go around and attend United Methodist churches, what strikes me is the way in which most of them (not all) are limited by what passes for possible in this world. United Methodists do not expect God's Spirit to intervene in powerful ways—to win the battle for us. As a result, we are resigned to the way things are. The logic of limited possibilities has seduced us. Perhaps this is because we are so comfortable with the way things are. If change is to take place, it will take place in the same old ways through the institutions of this world. The result has been compromise.

United Methodism has lost the sense of its own significance beyond the measures of worldly success. Methodism's awareness of its kingdom significance, both present and future, declined as its worldly significance increased, and we are confused. I remember being at Annual conference a couple of years ago and hearing it said, more than once, that the church exists "to serve the world." I can scarcely imagine a less correct interpretation of the church's mission. Jesus' kingdom is not of this world (Jn 18:36) and we serve him.

I said earlier that if we catch John Wesley's vision, the theology and the practices of Methodism come together. They make sense. The reverse is also true. Once we lose the vision, everything falls apart. It leaves us with an embarrassing language of salvation and with structures that no longer make any sense. In Wesley's sermon, "On Satan's Devices" he wrote:

> Our eye may be insensibly turned aside from that crown which the righteous Judge hath promised to give at that day "to all that love his appearing;" and we may be drawn away from the view of that incorruptible inheritance which is

reserved in heaven for us. But this also would be a loss to our souls, and an obstruction to our holiness. For to walk in the continual sight of our goal, is a needful help in our running the race that is set before us. ("On Satan's Devices," *Works*, [Jackson], vol. 6.)

United Methodism has stumbled in that race. We have taken our eye off the goal, and are drifting sophomorically toward an indeterminate future. We need to seek God's future, but more importantly, we need to receive it.

Chapter Three

A Message

Why Our Understanding of Salvation Matters

John Wesley's vision of the presence and possibility of God's kingdom, and of our lives conforming to the will of God, drove his understanding of what it means to be "saved" in this life. Full salvation and the message of grace provided the content of Methodist preaching. Most United Methodists have ignored the fullness of that message, and thus it has little impact in the world. We, and the world God loves, are no longer being saved in the full sense that Wesley used it, because we do not expect to be.

In the popular mind today, being saved has been reduced to being "born again," "having our sins forgiven," "being accepted by God." The problem is we live in a society that is not overly anxious about sin, either individual or societal. When we look at the lyrics to our popular music, the content of our popular television shows, the actions of our politicians, even the contents of our garages and refrigerators, it is pretty evident. Americans will do anything, say anything, consume anything in the pursuit of the measures of worldly happiness. We are not a shameful society. We are more accurately a shameless one.

People in societies defined primarily by consumer capitalism are not walking around wondering what they can do to win the approval of an angry God. We live in a culture of entitlement. We simply assume, no matter how we live, that God should accept us.

Even when people recognize they are not living how they should, the offer of God's forgiveness and acceptance has very little impact. People are more likely to think, "Why wouldn't God forgive me? My sins deserve forgiveness as much as the next persons. Of course God loves me. I'm lovable."

The good news is that the Wesleyan heritage, drawing on both Eastern and Western Christian traditions, offers us a model of salvation that is more than simply being born again, or being forgiven. That is part of it, but only part. A recovery of the fullness of the Wesleyan view of salvation will reinvigorate our practice of evangelism in ways that are biblically more faithful, theologically more sound, and practically more fruitful.

A Wesleyan Model for Salvation

One Sunday I was called upon to teach Sunday school to first and second graders at Hyattsville First United Methodist Church where my family has our membership. I do not usually teach this class. All I know is that the regular teacher and substitute were unable to come at the last minute and the first stand-in (i.e., the first one pressed to teach) was directing the youth choir that morning. She begged me to take the class.

I was thankful that at least I was to teach a story I was well acquainted with—the story of the prodigal son.(Lk 15:11-32.) As you know, in the story the younger son decided he was big enough to make his own decisions and demanded release from the care of his father. "Oh, and by the way Dad, I would like my inheritance too. Now, please. I don't want to have to wait until you are dead." This is a person with a sense of entitlement.

I asked my first and second graders what would happen if they talked to their parents the way that son talked to his dad. I wont share with you their responses. I'll tell you what though, you can learn a lot about people from what their kids say in Sunday school.

You can imagine how a parent would react if asked such a thing by a young adult. I know what my father would have said. And I know what I would say as a father. I would think my child had lost his mind. "No, of course you may not take half my net worth to run off and do what you want."

But in what has to be the most bizarre act of non-coercive parenting in the history of stories about familial relationships, this seemingly irresponsible father says, "Yes, here you go son. Take it. No, no, I'll manage." And off the son goes.

Most of you know the rest of the story. The son leaves home and country, blows all his money in riotous living, ends up working for a pig farmer (the lowest of the low employment for a good Kosher Jewish boy) and is so hungry he wants to eat pig slop. At this point in the story, he decides to return home and ask his father if he can be a servant. As he approaches the house, that irresponsible father runs out to meet him. Before the kid can get out his prepared speech, the father welcomes him as a son. The son is then restored to the household.

As I was teaching this story to six and seven year olds, it occurred to me what a great illustration it is for a Wesleyan understanding of salvation. Now many of you may be saying to yourselves, there is nothing particularly Wesleyan about that story. All Christians use that story. It is, after all, Jesus' story.

True, that story is used by all Christians. Yes, most Christians use it to illustrate something about salvation. Sin is forgiven in the story. But that is not what is most important about the story.

The story is a parable, which is a particular type of literature. It is not simply an allegory. A parable has something about it that challenges our view of reality. It is a story that forces us either to write it off as a load of nonsense or to rethink our understanding of the world.

What makes this particular parable a parable, what makes it both instructive and confusing, what gives it its literary power, is also the linchpin of a Wesleyan understanding of salvation.

The Character of God

The oddness of this story, its transformative focus, is not the character of the younger son (we have all met one or two of those guys in our day). Rather it is the character of the Father. The story is about the non-coercive, ever-present love of the father. It is a love that seems downright irresponsible—a love that is constant in all circumstances. It is a love that desires the happiness of the one who is loved while at the same time preserving the freedom of one who is loved—even the freedom to reject that love.

That kind of love (which is frankly far beyond that of any parent I have ever known) is the beginning point of any Wesleyan discussion of salvation. This love, for a Wesleyan, is the very character of God. Any presentation of God's interaction with God's creatures that obscures this character is not a true picture of the God who created us.

This was Wesley's chief objection to those whose understanding of salvation implied a hyper-Calvinist version of predestination. "So ill do election and reprobation agree with the truth and sincerity of God!" He wrote:

But do they not agree least of all with the scriptural account of his love and goodness? That attribute which God peculiarly claims, wherein he glories above all the rest. It is not written, "God is justice," or "God is truth:" (Although he is just and true in all his ways:) But it is written, "God is love," love in the abstract, without bounds; and "there is no end of his goodness." His love extends even to those who neither love nor fear him. He is good, even to the evil and the unthankful; yea, without any exception or limitation, to all the children of men. For "the Lord is loving" (or good) "to every man, and his mercy is over all his works." ("Predestination Calmly Considered," *Works* [Jackson], vol. 10.)

God's love extends over all of God's works, most particularly over the creatures made in God's image. A God who sent Christ to die only for some, who damns portions of creation for self-glory, is not, Wesley believed, the God revealed in Scripture.

This is important for Wesley, because until we know who God is, until we know the depth with which we are loved, we cannot really love God. And for Wesley, our salvation depends on our ability to love. Indeed, the degree to which we love God and neighbor is the degree to which we are saved.

God's love extends universally but God's love forces none. If it did it would cease to be love. Those who reject God's love may do so. That son could have starved there amidst the pig slop. But the point is, he need not, and his father does not want him to. *The father, in love, has limited his power over the son so that the son might know the depth with which he is loved and be empowered to love freely.*

Wesleyans have not made much of this distinctiveness at least since about the middle of the nineteenth century. We have not been willing to contend for an understanding of salvation that looks different from our fellow Protestants.

Part of the reason is how we understand the nature of the Church. The Church is not about opinions; the Church is about love. Thus, any unnecessary quibbling over opinions that does damage to the unity of love is at cross-purposes with God. We have been fond of quoting Wesley on just this point, if not actually living it.

But that is not the whole story for why we have been silent. Truth be told, we Wesleyans have forgotten what we mean by salvation. We have lost our boldness because we don't know why we should be bold. We have instead become known for throwing revivals or promoting social causes related to salvation. We have left the conversation about salvation *per se* to be dominated by others. And what has resulted is a shallow understanding of what it means to be saved.

The real scandal is that those other matters related to salvation—like justice for the oppressed and freedom of conscience—do not make sense outside of a particular understanding of what God desires for humanity and the means by which God is working to bring that about.

The Human Condition

To understand what we mean by salvation, we first need to understand our human condition. From what and for what are we being saved?

In Wesley's understanding of creation, God created purely out of love. God did not create out of a need to display God's glory. Creation was not about God, but about us. God created to make God's love material, to incarnate it. And God's attitude toward God's creation, towards us, is pure benevolence. God desires God's creatures, especially us humans, to be happy, to be lovingly blessed, as God is in God's Triune self. "For what end did God create man?" wrote Wesley,

> [The Westminster Assembly's] answer is, "To glorify and enjoy him forever." This is undoubtedly true; but is it quite clear, especially to men of ordinary capacities? Do the generality of common people understand that expression, "to glorify God"? No, no more than they understand Greek. And it is altogether above the capacity of children, to whom we can scarce ever speak plain enough. Now is not this the very principle that should be inculcated upon every human creature, "you are made to be happy in God"? . . . "He made you; and he made you to be happy in him; and nothing else can make you happy." ("The Unity of the Divine Being," *Works*, [Jackson] vol. 7.)

My guess is there are precious few people in our society wandering around asking themselves, "Am I glorifying God?" I hope there are a few, at least, reading this book. However, I am convinced there are plenty of people, in the suburbs, in the country, in the city, shopping at Wal-Mart, sitting in their cars, even pretending to listen as they sit in the pews of our churches, who are asking themselves, "Am I happy?" "Is this the life I was meant to live?" "What do I need to be truly happy?"

On the one hand, because we are created in the image of God, we have the tools we need to be happy.

> The Lord God . . . "created man in his own image" . . . endued with understanding. . . also endued with will, with various affections . . . that he might love, desire, and delight in that which is good; . . . likewise endued with liberty, a power of choosing what was good, and refusing what was not so. ("The End of Christ's Coming," Works, [Jackson], vol. 6.)

God created us to know, desire, and choose what will make us happy. And yet we don't make the choice. There is something radically wrong with us. Wesley has no trouble talking about the "entire depravity" of human beings in our "natural state." Left to our own devices we are completely hopeless, looking for love, looking for happiness, but only in the wrong places. We think that if we finally succeed the way the world defines it, we will be happy. If we finally have the cars and the houses of our dreams, or the recognition we deserve at work, or our fifteen minutes of fame, or the right spouse, we will be happy. Such is the message we receive 24/7 from the world around us. It drives our economy.

We, like the younger son, have left our father's house and have gone into a distant country. We are consuming our inheritance in eating and drinking. As long as the party lasts, we give not a thought toward our Father. We may even think for a time that we have found happiness. But we are wrong. We are confused. We are depraved. We are trapped. Without the assistance of God, we will never use our liberty in such a way that it leads us to real happiness, we will never understand or desire or choose what will make us happy. That assistance comes in the form of God's love, which is grace.

Grace

When that young man made the foolish decision to demand his inheritance before he was ready to deal with it wisely and before his father was dead, his father's love was extended to him. When that young man was spending his inheritance on things that would not endure, his father's love was still extended to him. When that young man was lost in a blur of alcohol and parties, his father's love was extended to him. When the money ran out and he was abandoned by everyone who had benefited from his flagrant spending, his father's love was still extended to him. Before he recognized it, his father's love was extended to him.

According to Wesley, the grace of God and the love of God are the same thing. Grace is God's love. In his sermon, "The Witness of Our Own Spirit," Wesley said that the grace of God is "that free love, that unmerited mercy, by which I a sinner, through the merits of Christ, am now reconciled to God." (*"Works*, [Jackson], vol. 5.)

And this grace, this love, is free. "The grace or love of God," wrote Wesley, "whence cometh our salvation, is free in all, and free for all." ("Free Grace," 2, *Works*, [Jackson], vol. 7.) That love is extended to all humanity regardless. No person is excluded for any reason. This grace, this love, indeed God's Holy Spirit is always present, surrounding us at every moment and pressing us toward its source, where we will find true happiness. The question is not whether grace is there, but what it is doing. How is grace working in us and in others?

Grace Is Preventing

Albert Outler introduced the term "prevenient" into the lexicon of Methodist theology. Wesley never used the term. Wesley's term was "preventing" grace. One could easily ask why would we replace a simple common word like "preventing" (the meaning of which is clear) with a twelve-dollar word like "prevenient," which no one but a specialist in theology can understand.

Outler's argument was that the meaning of the word "preventing" had changed since the eighteenth century and that use of the old term was confusing. Outler thought Wesley simply meant by preventing grace that grace comes before. This is certainly true of grace—the unmerited love of God does come before [*pre veni*] we do anything. Grace is there ahead of us, waiting for us, running out to meet us. But this is true of grace as it prevents, convinces, justifies, or sanctifies.

The problem is that the new term changes the part of speech. *Prevenient* is an adjective and describes a type of grace. It no longer describes what grace is doing—preventing.

What is grace then preventing?

In Wesley's sermon "The Image of God," which he included in the *Standard Sermons*, he describes the way in which humanity "lost the image of God" through disobedience.

> The liberty of man necessarily required that he should have some trial; else he would have had no choice whether he would stand or no, that is, no liberty at all. In order to this necessary trial God said to him, "Of every tree of the garden thou mayst freely eat, but of the tree of the knowledge of good and evil, thou shalt not eat of it." To secure him from transgressing this sole command, as far as could be done without destroying his liberty, the consequence was laid before him: "In the day that thou eatest thereof thou shalt surely die." Yet man did eat of it, and the consequence accordingly was death on him and all his descendents, and preparatory to death, sickness and pain, and folly and vice and slavery. And 'tis easy to observe by what regular steps all these would succeed each other, if God did not miraculously *prevent* it. ("The Image of God,

"*Works*, [Outler] vol. 4.)

God prevents the full natural consequences of creation's rebellion because of love. Wesley is clear that in rebellion, humanity has exchanged the image of God for the image of the devil. God could justly walk away from creation, as the father in our story could justly say, "You want me dead, you want your inheritance, then you are dead to me, we'll see how you do." That would be just, but it would not be God. God does not defend God's rights.

If God were to stop actively loving God's alienated fallen creation, there would be no hope of reconciliation, no hope of redemption. Instead, God chooses to actively love that which is not lovely. God's Spirit still strives with this broken old creation to bring about the possibility of recreation—a new creation. This striving of God's Holy Spirit with us is what Wesley believes accounts for the human conscience.

God's grace prevents the natural consequence of being out of God's will.

This brings us again to our younger son, at the beginning of our story. His fallen understanding has led him to think that he will find happiness outside of the restrictions of his father's household. Indeed as I mentioned before, as far as his own happiness is concerned, the father could just as well be dead. The son's will is determined to pursue his own happiness however he sees fit.

Off he goes to eat and drink and carouse his way to

happiness. He is, as Charles Wesley, John's brother, wrote, "a sinner satisfied in his sins; contented to remain in his fallen state, to live and die without the image of God; one who is ignorant both of his disease; and of the only remedy for it . . . ." ("Awake, Thou that Sleepest," *Works*, [Jackson], vol. 5.)

And yet, this young man as he drowned every thought of his father in riotous living, had, at every moment, the possibility of responding to the extended love of his father. That free love makes his salvation possible, prevents it from being impossible.

But for him to take advantage of that possibility would take some convincing, an action of grace Wesley sometimes includes under graces preventing work.

Grace Is Convincing

That convincing would come, as it often does, through seemingly terrible circumstances. As the story of the son goes, when the money ran out, so did his friends. As if that were not bad enough a famine takes place throughout the land, and his means of shielding himself from its effects are already gone. He winds up in circumstances he never thought he could be in. Death is close at hand. And he knows, is convinced, that it is time to make a change.

Convincing grace brought him to that point. Convincing grace is the unmerited love of God that presses us to recognize the pathetic state we are in. It is what gives us eyes to see that despite our pursuit of happiness on our own terms we have not, in fact, arrived at it. It is the beginning of the recognition of the vast gap between the love of God that has been offered to us and our rejection of it.

And so, younger son is brought to repentance. The Scriptures say, "he came to himself." In the words of the Wesley brothers, he woke up.

Grace Is Justifying

Once convinced, God's grace immediately begins to work to bring us to justification—seeks to reconcile us to God. The son knows he does not deserve to be a son, but something makes this young man think that he is not wholly repugnant to his father. If there is justice, his prospects in his father's house are limited. But he is counting on his father's mercy. Perhaps he could be a servant.

> "I will get up and go to my father, and I will say to him, 'Father, I have sinned against heaven and before you; I am no longer worthy to be called your son; treat me like one of your hired hands.'" (Lk 15:18-19.)

He has what Wesley would call "the faith of a servant." There is the realization of the unmerited love his father extends to him, but perhaps it only goes so far. The young man has a degree of faith in his father's love, but it is mixed with fear. How will his father's reaction when he sees him?

Even now, reconciliation with his father has begun, if only by the slightest degree. The son has, what Wesley described as, a degree of justifying faith.

The son with sorrow and hope now begins the journey back to his father's household, all the while rehearsing the speech he has written. "Father, I have sinned against heaven and before you; I am no longer worthy to be called your son; treat me like one of your hired hands."

In such a state of repentance, the grace of God, the unmerited love of God, seeks to restore our relationship to God, to reconcile us to God, to justify us before God. The unmerited love of God is extended to us in such a way as to expel all doubt that God has accepted us.

The faith of the young man, limited, timid though it is, is met with the overwhelming force of his father's free love. In opposition to all that traditional fathers should do and be, this father humbles himself and runs to his child. With an embrace he reveals his love, incarnates it, makes it real, tangible, and awesome.

"But while he was still far off," the Scriptures say, "his father saw him and was filled with compassion; he ran and put his arms around him and kissed him." (Lk 15:20) The son can barely get his prepared speech out and the father is already ordering a robe to clothe him, a ring for his finger, sandals for his feet, and a party to celebrate his homecoming.

Love has embraced him, love undeserved, love extended before he could get out his speech. Joy, unspeakable joy, fills his soul. He gets a taste of happiness, real happiness, as he has never known it before.

He is now assured of his father's love. He knows and trusts the depth of that love for him. He has experienced grace, as far beyond any sin he could imagine.

His conception of his father cannot help but be radically altered. He knows his father's character in a way he never did before. His father is not simply a kill-joy, not a stern disciplinarian who must be appeased. He is one who would give all, and still sacrifice more to win his child back.

So it is with us, when we, as Jesus says, "repent and believe." God meets us with love beyond what we deserve. God has humbled himself, made love incarnate, real, tangible, and awesome. It is a forgiveness we see in the one dying on the cross and when we can receive that embrace, in the language of Saint Paul, "[the] Spirit bearing witnesses with our spirit that we are children of God." (Rm 8:16.)

All things are different now. There is a new creation. This is a new life, not as a rebel, not as a servant, but as a child. Born again—free, really free, for the first time, to love the Father.

The son in our story is restored to the household, he is forgiven by his father, he is assured of his father's favor and his father's love, but there is still far more for him to learn about and from his father. His salvation is not complete.

Grace Is Sanctifying

For the unmerited love of God desires not simply that we be welcomed back into the family, but that we be healed of all that led us into misery in the first place. Salvation, in a Wesleyan context, is not simply forgiveness, it is not simply a get out of jail free card. Rather, it is the complete restoration of who we have been created to be, here and now, in this life.

> "We may learn . . . what is the proper nature of religion," wrote Wesley in his sermon on "Original Sin," "of the religion of Jesus Christ. It is [therapeia psycheis], God's method of healing a soul which is thus diseased." ("Original Sin," *Works*, [Jackson], vol. 6.)

God is extending God's love to us, not so that the Trinity would have more company in heaven. God extends God's love to us so that we might grow into the mature character of the free love that has embraced us.

Now that we are part of the household of God, God's unmerited love draws us more fully into who we have been remade to be. It sanctifies us, makes us into saints, leads us into real, substantial happiness, not based on the externals of our circumstances, but on the unmerited love of God in Christ Jesus. We become like the love that has embraced us.

There is still work to be done on the farm. The same rules that chafed the son are still in place, though these are transformed by his new insight into his father. They are no longer arbitrary; they are means of conveying grace, his father's free love. They are marks of his membership in the family, tools to help him be truly happy.

Living into them increases his knowledge of the one who instituted them. Living into them is an expression of love toward his father as he has been loved. Living into them will teach him to love others as himself.

That is not to say that life in the household is free from conflict. If you know the rest of the story of the Prodigal Son, you know that is not the case. Like in that story, there is sibling rivalry, there are hurt feelings. Even those who have not sinned as boldly as the younger brother need to recognize the sheer gift that is being a child of God. In short, there is no end of opportunities to love even the unlovely, just as we were loved.

Through these trials, the image of God is gradually restored in us, and we are led to pursue happiness where it is to be found. "Thus it is," wrote Wesley, "by manifesting himself, he destroys the works of the devil, restoring the guilty outcast from God to his favour, to pardon and peace; the sinner in whom dwelleth no good thing, to love and holiness; the burdened, miserable sinner, to joy unspeakable, to real, substantial happiness." ("The End of Christ's Coming," *Works*, [Jackson], vol. 6.)

Conclusion

Unlike other conceptions of salvation that frame it as simply the forgiveness of sins at a moment in time, or a decision that writes our name in permanent ink in the Book of Life, or what will happen to us beyond the grave, a Wesleyan understanding of salvation is of something that happens over time. It begins before we even realize it and continues until we are perfected in Love. It is something we live into and work out here and now.

We cannot earn our salvation. It is founded in, and at every moment moved forward by, grace—the free love of God. However, we can work with that grace. Salvation is a process of human beings responding to the ever-present love of God, responding to grace extended to the chief of sinners.

"What is *salvation?*" Wesley wrote. "The salvation which is here spoken of is not what is frequently understood by that word, the going to heaven . . . It is not a blessing which lies on the other side of death . . . it is a present thing . . . [it] might be extended to the entire work of God, from the first dawning of grace in the soul till it is consummated in glory." ("Scripture Way of Salvation," *Works*, [Jackson], vol. 6.)

The rhetoric of America includes the inalienable rights of life, liberty, and the pursuit of happiness. These things God desires for us as well. But most people in our society are engaged in an impossible task, seeking them where they are not to be found. Do we have something to say to those who are weary with toil, and storing up goods, and making the world safe for consumption? I believe we do, and it is much more than getting to go to heaven when they die.

What we have to offer is a way, we would say "the Way." The way back home, the way of full salvation by grace, the way to authentic happiness. It is a way made possible by God's love to humanity, revealed in God's love incarnate, through the power of God's love always surrounding us.

Chapter Four

A Method

The United Methodist Church currently engages in a multitude of activities to reach individuals for Christ and transform society, but it undergirds them with very few theological principles. If we peal back the veneer of God talk, most of what passes for outreach or witness in our denomination has, at best, a bankrupt vision of God's purpose for creation and a truncated understanding of salvation. At worst, we find practices that are little more than thinly veiled attempts to manipulate others through politics or marketing techniques—practices that owe more to the myth of western progress and the ethics of consumer capitalism than they do to the gospel.

Our efforts at discipleship are similarly diffuse. Membership is largely decided by local whim. Confirmation, Sunday school classes, prayer meetings, covenant groups, and any number of different small group activities and programs, change with dizzying regularity. We claim we want to "make disciples," but we have no guide for knowing when we have actually made one.

This was not true of early Wesleyan methodology. The practices of the Methodist Movement were theologically grounded in Wesley's understanding of God's character and the ways God's grace is active, working to save God's beloved creatures.

Christ in All His Offices

Wesley never separated faith and works, what we believe about Christ from what we do in Christ. Our doctrine and our discipline were consistent. For this reason, Wesley insisted that his evangelists preach Christ in "all his offices"—as prophet, priest, and king. Methodism did not only preach forgiveness of sins through the sacrifice of Christ, or even the new birth— Jesus our great high priest. Methodism proclaimed the fullness of the incarnate Word a full gospel—Jesus our prophet and our king.

> We are not ourselves clear before God, unless we proclaim [Christ] in all his offices. To preach Christ, as a workman that needeth not to be

ashamed, is to preach him, not only as our great
High Priest, . . . but likewise as the Prophet of the
Lord, . . . yea, and as remaining a King for ever; . . .
until he hath utterly cast out all sin, and brought in
everlasting righteousness. ("Law Established
Through Faith," *Works*, [Jackson], vol. 5.)

The various ways God's grace ministers to humanity
convincing, justifying, and sanctifying, corresponds to
Christ's offices of prophet, priest, and king. For Wesley, it
was not enough to minister with the convincing grace of
God, with Christ as prophet, letting people know they
are on the wrong path, that God desires something more
for them. It was not enough to minister only with the
justifying grace of God, with Christ as priest, preaching
forgiveness to people before they knew they needed it. It
was not enough to minister with God's sanctifying grace,
with Christ as king, encouraging holy living. Proclaiming
the full gospel meant proclaiming the full Christ.
Methodism existed, as Wesley wrote, "to convince the
gainsayer; to direct their feet into the way of peace, and
then keep them therein" ("A Farther Appeal to Men of
Reason and Religion," *Works* [Jackson], vol. 8.)—to convince, to justify, to sanctify.

The Methodist movement ordered its life to serve this
mission. Wesley wrote to John Smith, "What is the aim
of any ecclesiastical order? Is it not to snatch souls from
the power of Satan for God and to edify them in the love
and fear of God? Order, then has value only if it
responds to these aims; and if not, it is worthless."

(*Works* [Jackson], vol. 12, pp. 80-81.)

Methodist practice was consistent with its theology. Methodism worked with God's grace to bring people into the fullness of the religion of Jesus Christ—the love of God and neighbor—which is their true home. Wesley wrote:

> Our main doctrines, which include all the rest, are three,—that of repentance, of faith, and of holiness. The first of these we account, as it were, the porch of religion; the next, the door; the third, religion itself. ("The Principles of a Methodist Farther Explained" *Works* [Jackson], vol. 8.)

Christ came to create a people of transformed and transforming lives who are a witness to the power of his resurrection and his reign—a holy priesthood. Helping people on the porch, through the door, and into the house, was God's desire and Methodism's charge.

Open-Air Preaching: Grace Convincing Us

Methodism's first task was to help people onto the porch. The foundational structure for working with God's convincing grace was preaching in the open air, not in a church or any building. The market place was Wesley's most frequently used post for this preaching—often the market cross. This stone monument at the center of a market town provided symbolic focus for the intersection of the sacred with the secular. Here the salvation of God met the everyday lives of the people. Here consumers, thieves, merchants, slaves, saints and sinners gathered for the business of the day.

Here the Methodists were also present with a message of God's full salvation.

Throughout his ministry, Wesley could not stress enough the importance of meeting ordinary people on their own turf with the message of God's work of salvation. "I preached to a large and very serious congregation on Redcliff-Hill," wrote Wesley. "This is the way to overturn Satan's kingdom. In field-preaching, more than any other means, God is found of them that sought him not. By this, death, heaven, and hell, come to the ears, if not the hearts, of them that 'care for none of these things.'" (*Journal* from May 27, 1765 to May 5, 1768," *Works* [Jackson], vol. 3.)

Wesley did not invent this practice. Preaching outside of a church was a method that had been used by independents, Quakers, and other "socially unacceptable" groups for years. Wesley's former student George Whitfield, the son of a tavern keeper, had taken it up. But it was quite another thing for an Oxford don to do the same. As I mentioned in chapter one, on April 2, 1739, a year after his heart-warming experience, Wesley preached in the Bristol brickyard and Wesley's bold humiliation gave birth to the Wesleyan Methodist revival.

Throughout his ministry, Wesley's general practice was to preach out of doors, to whoever would listen, at least twice a day. He believed that if this work ceased, so would revival. "It is the cooping yourselves up in rooms" he wrote in a letter to James Rea in 1766, "that has damped the work of God, which never was and never will be carried out to any purpose without going out into the highways and hedges and compelling poor sinners to come in."("Letter to James Rea, July 21, 1766," *Works* [Jackson], vol. 5.)

Toward the end of his career Wesley noted with sadness,

> In the evening I preached at Stroud; where, to my surprise, I found the morning preaching was given up, as also in the neighbouring places. If this be the case while I am alive, what must it be when I am gone? Give up this, and Methodism too will degenerate into a mere sect, only distinguished by some opinions and modes of worship. (*Journal* from September 4, 1782 to June 28, 1786" *Works* [Jackson], vol. 4.)

In our generation, we must find the equivalent of the Market Cross if we are to regain our evangelistic vitality. Where and how do we to submit ourselves to be *more vile* to reach those who will not cross the thresholds of our churches? We must find the places where ideas are exchanged at the level of the common person and we must be present in those forums. But even if we find that place where we can communicate to those who may not enter one of our buildings, we need to know what to say.

In "market cross" sermons, Methodists intentionally cooperated with God's convincing grace, the prophetic office of Christ. This kind of preaching began with

God's preventing grace, "a general declaration of the love God to sinners, and his willingness that they should be saved." ("Letter on Preaching Christ," *Works* [Jackson], vol. 11.) However, the message did not end there. The goal was to wake people up publicly to the hollowness of their search for happiness—to the reality of their separation from what will make them truly happy—from God.

Here the Church worked with God's free love to convince those to whom it is extended that where they're looking for happiness is actually distancing them from God and real happiness. In old-fashioned terms, we invite people to turn around—to repent. This was not a message tailored to what an audience would like to hear. This was not marketing for God. . It was a message that began with people's real need to be convinced of their need.

Wesley was no respecter of persons. He recounts in his *Journal*. "At four I preached at the Shire-Hall of Cardiff again, where many gentry, I found, were present. Such freedom of speech I have seldom had, as was given me in explaining those words, 'The kingdom of God is not meat and drink; but righteousness, and peace, and joy in the Holy Ghost.'" (*Journal*, *Works* [Jackson], vol. 1.)

The effect of open-air "market cross" preaching was often quite dramatic. Tom Albin recounts the experience of John Garritt (1756-1841) who told his story of God's grace in the pages of Wesley's *Arminian Magazine*. He wrote:

1773, when I was about 17 years of age I providentially heard a Methodist preacher, namely Mr. Bardsly. His text was Isaiah 3:10. "Say ye to the righteous, it shall be well with him for he shall eat the fruit of his doings. Woe to the wicked. It shall be ill with him for the reward of his hands shall be given him.' I went home weeping and continued to weep and pray for near a month. Praying that the Lord would save me from hell, for at that time I was ignorant of the plan of salvation by faith in Christ." (Tom Albin, "An Empirical Study of Early Methodist Spirituality," *Wesleyan Spirituality Today* [Nashville: United Methodist Publishing House, 1985], 275-6.)

Such prophetic work was never popular, never easy. Early on, Methodist preachers faced mobs and even death. It took courage. It took humility. Even Wesley, as late as the 1770s wrote, "I preached on the quay, at Kingswood, and near King's Square. To this day field-preaching is a cross to me. But I know my commission, and see no other way of 'preaching the Gospel to every creature.'"(*Journal* from September 2, 1770 to September 12, 1773 *Works* [Jackson], vol. 3.) Wesley insisted his preachers preach to the masses so that the Methodists might work with God's grace from the beginning, to convince all people to stop their fruitless search for happiness and turn to God. And because of this work, at least, one John Garritt mounted the porch.

The Class Meeting: Grace Justifying Us

Those who responded at the market cross always had an opportunity for further response. At the start of the Methodist work in Newcastle, Wesley concluded his first field sermon on Isaiah 53:3 with, "If you desire to know who I am, my name is John Wesley. At five in the evening, with God's help, I design to preach here again." (*Journal*, May 30, 1742, *Works*, [Jackson], vol. 1.) Often, members of the local society would be in attendance at field preaching to discern those who were touched by the message and invite them to a later preaching service, either out of doors or to join the society. Garritt wrote of his experience:

> I went to hear again and the preacher was Mr. Thomas Taylor. . . . In this discourse he told us that all by nature were unacquainted with the Lord and had no true peace. He proceeded to preach to us how we might become acquainted with the Lord so as to find pardon and peace. I was much enlightened by his discourse and joined the society. (Albin, "Empirical Study," 275-6.)

Joining the society was no easy handshake at the front of the church. Membership in the society meant being part of a class meeting—a small group where one began to talk about one's spiritual state and was expected to begin to live as a disciple, which meant submitting to discipline. Because this was a serious matter, people were admitted to membership on trial for a period of several weeks, to see if they were truly willing to live under discipline.

Wesley was reinventing the practice of the catechumenate—a time, in the ancient church, prior to baptism where one was taught what it means to be a Christian disciple. Wesley, though he was dealing with a baptized culture, understood that fellowship exists among disciples. Thus, without discipline, there is no real fellowship.

Wesley first published the "General Rules" in 1743 as a set of guidelines for the societies as a whole. Printed as a small penny pamphlet that nearly anyone could afford, the Rules went through thirty nine editions in his lifetime. The rules were succinct and specific guidance for anyone trying to live like a disciple. They were simple, understandable, and holistic.

The first rule was: *Do No Harm.* It went on to read that Methodists were to avoid evil of "every kind—especially that which is most generally practiced." Then follows a long list of many types of evil prevalent in Wesley's day.

The second rule was: *Do Good.* These were works of mercy, reflections of God's free unmerited love to others. This involved meeting the physical, spiritual, and social needs of those around us, as well as being concerned for larger issues that harm our neighbor. It also included "submitting to bear the reproach of Christ, to be as 'the filth and offscouring of the world.'"

The third rule was: *Attend the Ordinances of God.* This included both the public and private acts of piety, "The public worship of God: the ministry of the Word, whether read or expounded; the Supper of the Lord; private prayer; searching the Scriptures; and Fasting, or abstinence."

To aid accountability, all members of the society were part of a class. These groups were limited to twelve members, and were instituted at least partly for a practical purpose, to aid in the collection subscriptions for the building of the New Room in Bristol. However, they also served a spiritual end.

In the classes, "Many now happily experienced that Christian fellowship of which they had not so much as an idea before. They began to 'bear one another's burdens', and 'naturally' to 'care for each other.'" (Plain Account II, *Works*, [Jackson] vol. 8.)

In the class, one's penitence was met with the hospitality of the body of Christ. Tom Albin's research into the salvation narratives that appeared in the *Arminian Magazine* showed that the majority of experiences of the new birth happened *after* membership in the class meeting, at times in the meetings themselves.(Albin, Empirical Study, 275-6.) One was part of a small disciplined community seeking and expecting the grace of God before one experienced it for oneself.

The class meeting was so central to the ministry of Methodism that Wesley vowed not to preach where it was absent. "I am more and more convinced," he wrote early in his ministry, "that the devil himself desires nothing more than this, that the people of any place should be half-awakened, and then left to themselves to fall asleep again. Therefore I determine, by the grace of God, not to strike one stroke in any place where I cannot follow the blow." (*Journal* from September 3, 1741 to October 27, 1743, *Works*, [Outler], vol. 19.)

Contemporary study after study has shown that seekers first need to know they belong, before they come to believe. Like with the early Church's practice of the chatecumenate, faith is born in the midst of relationship. The class meeting was central to making Christians because through it the church cooperated with the justifying grace of God, welcoming the sinner and embracing them with the love of God.

This is illustrated again in the testimony of John Garritt:

> The first time I met in class my knowledge of the plan of salvation through Jesus Christ was much increased. I prayed at all opportunities, in the house, barn, and fields; and I soon found peace with God and sang;
>
> Ah wherefore did I ever doubt,
> Thou wilt in nowise cast me out.
> A helpless soul that comes to thee
> With only sin and misery. 1774
> (Albin, "Empirical Study," 275-6.)

Garritt came to know the free love God extended in order to justify him. He received a faith that implies "a sure confidence in God that through the merits of Christ his sins are forgiven, and he reconciled to the favour of God."("The Marks of the New Birth," *Works*, [Jackson], vol. 5.) By this faith all things were made new, he saw the face of a loving God and the penitent sinner was born again. Garritt had entered the door.

The class meeting is little more than a memory within most quarters of Methodism. As the church has become more mainstream, more comfortable with the surrounding culture, it has become less willing to be different, to be disciplined. Perhaps it is not possible to recover the class meeting as it was for our present day. But if our ministry is to be effective in the present age, we must recover what they provided: small, disciplined, hospitable, caring fellowships for non-Christians and Christians alike. Without them the larger church loses our witness, our community, our cooperation with the justifying grace of God, and ultimately our ability to help people be born into the reign of God.

The Band Meeting: Grace Sanctifying Us

As Wesley understood it, God's work of salvation is not completed when one is born again. A new believer needs to be led into the fullness of what has been tasted—the fullness of the good news, the fullness of Christ. A new believer needs to experience what it is to live daily in the love of God. Once the "faith of a child" is begotten, the promised witness of the Spirit received, a believer has crossed the threshold into the house. However, living in the house is no simple matter.

God's mission was not complete and so neither was that of the Methodists. For Wesley, fostering holiness, making saints, was part of the same ministry of salvation through faith in the Gospel of Christ. Only now the work of God's people cooperated with the God's grace as it sanctifies us.

Those who had experienced the new birth could be "divided . . . into smaller companies; putting married or single men, and married or single women together." Here people could deal with "temptations of such a kind as they knew not how to speak in a class [where] persons of every sort, young and old, men and women, met together." ("A Plain Account of the People Called Methodist, *Works*, [Jackson], vol. 8.) For though they had experienced the new birth, their salvation was not yet complete. Sin still had power, though it did not reign. As Wesley wrote, "for the war was not over. . . . They had still to wrestle with flesh and blood, and with principalities and powers; so that temptations were on every side."

These band meetings, as Wesley called them, were intimate confession groups for those who had experienced the new birth. There, believers could, as Wesley wrote, "pour out of their hearts without reserve, particularly with regard to the sin which did still 'easily beset' them, and the temptations which were most apt to prevail over them." ("Plain Account," *Works*, [Jackson], vol. 8.) Through confession, the power of temptation and sin was disarmed. Believers learned to submit every dark corner of their lives to the kingly office of Christ.

To this end, the bands, which met weekly, also had rules. They read:

In order to "confess our faults one to another, and pray one for another that we may be healed" we intend: . . .To speak, each of us in order, freely and plainly, the true state of our soul, with the faults we have committed in thought, word, or deed, and the temptations we have felt since our last meeting. To desire some person among us (thence called a Leader) to speak his own state first, and then to ask the rest in order as many and as searching questions as may be, concerning their state, sins, and temptations. ("Plain Account," *Works*, [Jackson], vol. 8.)

Each week the members of the bands would answer five questions each in turn:

1. What sins have you committed since we last met?
2. What temptations have you met with?
3. How were you delivered?
4. What have you done that you know not if it be sin?
5. Have you any secrets?

To be part of a band meant being willing to shuck pretense, to be humble before a brother or sister in Christ. It meant acting as a priest one to another, acting in love toward another whose sin you know. It meant allowing someone, who knows your sin, to act in love toward you. It meant humility. It meant Christlikeness. It meant holiness.

That kind of honesty and integrity is tremendously rare in our society, which values superficial externals and "spin" so highly. Unfortunately, it is also tremendously rare within the contemporary Church. The band meeting was the church being truly counter-cultural—working on an extreme makeover from the inside out.

In the bands, people expected that through confession, God would fulfill God's promise to "heal them"—to "cleanse them from all unrighteousness." People expected that they could be finally and fully saved. People began to live radically for the kingdom of Christ, empowered by the love of Christ.

Conclusion

The structures of the Wesleyan Methodist revival were not "planned" from the outset, but they were not haphazard. They reflected theological commitments, which grew out of John Wesley's understanding of the character of God as love, of God's salvific work in Christ, and of God's grace furthering this work through the power and presence of the Holy Spirit.

Grace, God's free unmerited love extended to God's creatures, is working by convincing, justifying, and sanctifying us. Christ is ministering as to us as prophet, priest, and king. God is striving by the Holy Spirit to bring his children to the porch, through the door, and ultimately into the house of religion.

The very nature of God's salvation implies that God's people cooperate with God's grace every step of the way of salvation. Love of neighbor compels the church to work with God's love as it ministers in the world.

The work of God's people, as Wesley and the early Methodists understood it, was not to manipulate people into an institution—to increase attendance or fill the coffers of the church. Our work is to work with the grace of God because God is already working. True ministry reaches out to people in all spiritual circumstances by incarnating the love of God, revealed in Christ, by the power of the Holy Spirit.

With those asleep in sin, Methodism's missional task is to minister in Christ's prophetic office—publicly, in the open air, at the market cross—to convince people of their need for God. With those already convinced of their need for God, Methodism's missional task is to introduce them to the one who can meet that need—to their great high priest. With those who know God's forgiving love, Methodism's missional task is to work to save them from the power of sin—bring every part of their lives into the love of Christ the king.

The Church is called to assist where and how God's grace is moving. Wesley's practices of open air preaching, of class meetings, and of band meetings were expressions of these theological commitments. Together they formed a series of structures wherein those asleep in sin might be fully saved. And the Church was revived, and society reformed.

Our so-called Methodist church has largely given up on the sorts of structures by which we formerly cooperated with God's grace. Even when we attempt to recover some, it is generally a piecemeal effort. It is no wonder our efforts seem unfruitful.

If we, the Church, are to recover our vitality, if we are to become again a tool for God's transformation of society instead of a carrier of the myth of western progress, we must find practices that cooperate with God's grace at every stage of salvation.

We must become, as Wesley admonished, like "the Christians of old."

> They endeavoured herein to speak to every man severally as he had need. To the careless, to those who lay unconcerned in darkness and in the shadow of death, the thundered, "Awake, thou that sleepest, . . . arise from the dead, and Christ shall give thee light." But to those who were already awakened out of sleep, and groaning under a sense of the wrath of God, their language was, "We have an advocate with the Father; . . . he is the propitiation for our sins." Meantime those who had believed they "provoked to love and to good works"; to "patient continuance in well-doing"; and to "abound more and more" in that "holiness, without which no man can see the Lord". ("Scriptural Christianity," *Works*, [Jackson], vol. 5.)

Such practices will not be popular in or out of the Church. Such a recovery will not be easy. But we will be working with God, with Christ, and in the power of the Holy Spirit. And if we are with God, God will be with us.

Chapter Five

A Conversation

Have you ever dreaded a conversation?

A few years ago, I came into my office at Wesley Theological Seminary and I saw that there were several messages on my voice mail. I pushed the button to listen to the messages, while I turned on the computer to check my email. Two of the voicemails were in reference to the Bishop of my annual conference. One was from the bishop's office, asking me to contact the Bishop; the other was from the receptionist at Wesley, telling me my Bishop was looking for me. When my email came up, there it was—an email also alerting me that I needed to contact the Bishop's office.

Apparently he and I needed to have a conversation.

I made three calls. The first was to my wife, Roberta, telling her I was going to return a call to the Bishop. The second was to my Dean, telling him I was going to return a call to the Bishop. Then . . . I called the Bishop.

As it turned out, he only asked me to talk to our Annual Conference about "holy conferencing." I said yes, of course. I was so relieved I would have said yes to just about anything. But I need to confess that I did not say "yes" because of my great love for this institution of conferencing, at least as it now operates.

I didn't tell this to the Bishop, but asking me to talk about conferencing is a bit like asking cattle to talk about electric fences. I do not enjoy Conference. The whole thing, the atmosphere, the work we do, is not, for me, usually an experience of the reign of God. The energy I get for ministry, where I get connected to God and God's kingdom, happens elsewhere. Honestly, I usually leave annual conference depressed, more cynical, and sometimes angry.

Apparently God, through the Bishop, wanted me to deal with my "growing edges." So . . . conference.

Anyone looking in on what we now call conference must wonder what it is all about. Such events are very impressive. My annual conference is held in a basketball coliseum, which must be quite an expense. There is a ton of coordination that goes on—the work and planning by the conference staff, who execute these extravaganzas.

Then there is what actually goes on at these Conferences. We spend time in committees dealing with all of the legislation that different churches and interest groups have put on our plate for this year. We have some learning/training opportunities. We see a new group of people ordained to serve God as Deacons and Elders. We honor those who will cease active service, and those who have died over the past year. Finally, we get time away from your regular routine to reconnect with brothers and sisters in Christ, with whom we may have lost contact over the year.

It may surprise us then, that none of these activities is the reason conference was established as the guiding body of Methodism. None of these is the reason we call this event an annual *conference*.

The outlines of the story should be familiar to you if you have read the preceding chapters. In 1738, a high church Anglican, Oxford academic met Jesus for real and began acting very contrary to character. He lowered himself to preach outside of a church and to focus his attentions not on the promising young men in the university, but on the working class men and women struggling along in early industrial England.

He was not the only or even the first to have met Jesus like this. A movement of God's Spirit seemed to be sweeping Europe through all the confessions. New, enlivened Christians were forming societies in many parts of England and Europe. Gradually, this Oxford academic's idiosyncrasies, and theological distinctives, made him the overseer of two of such groups of enlivened believers in England—one in London, the other in Bristol.

His own sense of the Holy Spirit of God led him to allow some very un-high church Anglican, unacademic, things—like lay leadership and even lay preaching. Amazingly, the number of groups began to multiply and spread to new towns and communities.

Within four years of this movement's beginning under his leadership, John Wesley knew that he was in over his head. The little societies in London and Bristol had mutated into a small semi-monastic preaching order. He needed a tool to help him seek the Spirit's direction for this new order—he needed a means of grace. Wesley wrote:

> In June 1744, I desired my brother and a few other Clergymen to meet me in London, to consider how we should proceed to save our own souls and those that heard us. After some time, I invited the lay Preachers that were in the house to meet with us. We *conferred* together for several days, and were much comforted and strengthened thereby. The next year I not only invited most of the Traveling Preachers, but several others, to confer with me in Bristol. And from that time for some years, though I invited only a part of the Traveling Preachers, yet I permitted any that desired it, to be present . . . . This I did for many years, and all that time the term *Conference* meant not so much the conversations we had together, as the persons that conferred; namely, those whom I invited to confer with me from time to time. ("Thoughts Upon some Late Occurrences" 1785, *Works* [Jackson], vol. 13.)

What Is Conference?

A Conference is a group of people, selected for their spiritual wisdom and maturity, which confers together. A conference is not a group of people who legislate, who study, who ordain, who celebrate, or even who fellowship. Some of these may be legitimate things to do alongside conferring, but they are not supposed to be why they gather.

Conference gathered together those whose spiritual insights Wesley knew he needed, those he knew would be open to the leading of the Holy Spirit, to think, talk, and pray together as they sought God's direction. And if Wesley thought there were those liable to be especially obstreperous or hard headed, they were purposely not invited.

Conference does not begin with a motion; it begins with a question. Three overarching questions kept Conferences in Wesley's day grounded in the essentials of what God was doing. All questions to be conferred on related to three general questions.

1. What to teach;
2. How to teach;
3. What to do; that is, how to regulate our doctrine, discipline, and practice. (*Works* [Jackson] vol. 8, p. 275.)

Within these larger questions, specific questions, which had arisen in their day, would be addressed. These were questions on which the whole community needed clarity if they were to move forward with God's Spirit. We ask the question because we don't already know the answer.

The first conferences focused on questions we addressed in chapter three, questions about what it means to be saved—the way of salvation. What do we mean by justification and sanctification? What are the roles of grace and works in salvation? How do we understand the witness of the Holy Spirit? What is perfection?

Christian conferencing is not about a series of "whereas" clauses followed by a "therefore." If anything has killed off real conferencing, it is its confusion with legislating and the acceptance of lobbying in the process.

If you're familiar with conferences today, you probably thinking that we don't have time to really confer when we have so much business to take care of during the few days we have together. Why engage in what is ultimately a fruitless activity? We already know that we are not going to agree. Let's just get on with the voting, the seminars, the worship services. That attitude simply demonstrates how desperately we need to start having real conferences again.

In our current practice of "conferencing," we have adopted the means of the world instead of what was intended as a means of grace.

Why Confer?

We confer for one reason and one reason only. Because we are called to play a part in a movement of

God's Spirit. And that movement is big.

That movement began 2000 years ago with a few scared people huddled in an upper room in Jerusalem with a mission to Jerusalem, Judea, Samaria, and the end of the earth. That movement swept an eighteenth century high-church Oxford academic out of his ivory tower. Right now, that movement is sweeping through China, parts of Africa, and South and Central America, even Iran. That movement is giving people a taste of the kingdom of God in the person of Jesus Christ. That movement is bringing the arrogant to their knees and lifting up the poor, right now, today.

United Methodism matters only if it is connected to, a part of, that movement. If not, it is worthless, and might as well cease to exist. To make sure we are continuing to be part of that movement requires discernment. And discerning the Spirit of God requires a seeking community.

Can we recover that character—the character of a community truly seeking to understand what the reign of God demands? Can we really care less about our own opinions than about what God's will would look like were it done on earth as in heaven?

This will take a concerted effort on our parts. We will need to break the patterns of the world that we have fallen into and called "Conferencing."

The actual "Steps toward real Conferencing" I offer are nothing new. They do not come from me but from St. Paul. In the letter to the Ephesians, he writes:

I therefore, the prisoner in the Lord, beg you to lead a life worthy of the calling to which you have been called, with all humility and gentleness, with patience, bearing with one another in love, making every effort to maintain the unity of the Spirit in the bond of peace. (Ephesians 4:1-3.)

Humility, gentleness, patience, bearing with one another in love—these are the steps we must take to begin real conferencing.

STEP 1: HUMILITY

To begin real conferencing we will first each have to realize that none of us, on our own, perceives God's will perfectly.

Despite all of the images we have of John Wesley as a monarchial leader who ran his movement at the micro level and kept control of every aspect of its identity, the existence of conference points to another aspect of Wesley—*humility*.

Wesley knew that, alone, he did not have the ability to perceive what the Holy Spirit wanted. Yes, he had been "laid hold of" and "driven along" by God. Yes, God had used him in God's revival of Christianity in England. But Wesley knew God revealed himself primarily in community. He knew he needed others to discern God's will.

As fallen, sinful people, we are capable of all sorts of delusions and self-deceptions. Our different backgrounds, ethnic communities, social classes, and educations mold our perceptions. They give us blind spots. They also give us insight. Everyone called to conference, if he or she is seeking the Holy Spirit's guidance, has something to contribute.

Our conferencing has taken on the character of our American political debate. We simplify issues by dividing them into two extremes from which the rest of us are forced to choose. However, the danger of presenting "both sides" is that we then think we have been fair, as though the options for how to think and frame a given issue had been exhausted.

We gather as a body with many different perspectives because there are never only two sides to a question and never only one way to frame a question.

One example is our debate over homosexuality. The issue is often framed as a question of biblical authority. I, as a historian and not a biblical scholar, am skeptical. I suspect that this issue, and most of our most divisive issues, are not primarily about biblical authority. Methodists, after all, have never split over an issue of biblical interpretation, or over a particular doctrine of inspiration, or over doctrine at all.

Our many, many splits in our history (over the way bishops exercise their authority, the treatment of ethnic minorities, slavery, even pew rents) tend to be a reflection of our original mission—to reform the continent and spread scriptural holiness across the land. The questions Methodists have usually struggled with are: What does "scriptural holiness" look like? When is the Church conforming to the world?

Now, reframing the question does not answer it, but it does get us out of the worldly trap of dividing issues into two "extremes," and then polarizing a community. There are as many perspectives and possibilities present at a conference as there are fallen creatures there, made in the image of God and needing to be healed. That is a good thing.

I have opinions. But I could be wrong. And so could you. I need you to help me see my own blind spots and guide me toward the truth, toward righteousness. And you need me.

We must begin our conference where Jesus began the Sermon on the Mount, with the recognition of the spiritual poverty, of our own need for each other, our own need for those who may disagree with us initially, if we are to discern the will of God.

Step 2: Gentleness

If we are to really conference, we have to put down the tools of manipulation and coercion in relation to our brothers and sisters, and deal with each other as the fragile, pathetic, yet sacrificially loved creatures we are.

We need to stop thinking of what happens at conference as a win/lose proposition, where we engage in argument and lobbying to persuade and political maneuverings to succeed. I remember being at an annual conference luncheon organized by United Methodists for Renewal. The speaker, a young minister in that conference, confessed how, through all the business of ministry, he had "abandoned the love he had at first" (Rev 2:4). He called on all of us present to return to our first love. By the end of the talk, people were literally in tears, and the offer was made for people to come forward to pray for the conference, to confess and receive prayer for forgiveness and renewal. As soon as the altar call was made, as people began moving to the front, one of the organizers of the luncheon stood up to announce that voting for delegates was about to take place, and encouraging everyone not to tarry.

That was when I started weeping. We had received a visitation of the Lord that day and we deserted him for the world. If we Methodists are ever going to depend again on the Holy Spirit, all our parties will need to lay down our swords and shields, study war no more, and return to our first love.

It is sad beyond expression that at our annual conferences we so-called "followers of Christ" have to remind each other of what Christ-like conduct towards another is. We have become so used to conforming our patterns of conversation to the world's that our "conferring" more closely resemble a secular legislature, or worse still, the Jerry Springer show.

Prior to the previous General Conference, the United Methodist Church held several conversations entitled "In Search of Unity." These were probably the first instances of real, holy conferencing that had been attempted in a number of years. One of the best things to come out of those conversations was the "Guidelines for Civility." I prefer to think of them as "Guidelines for Ecclesiality."

They are as follows.

1. Respect the personhood of others, while engaging their ideas.
2. Carefully represent the views of those with whom we are in disagreement.
3. Be careful in defining terms, avoiding needless use of inflammatory words.
4. Be careful in the use of generalizations. Where appropriate, offer specific evidence.
5. Seek to understand the experiences out of which others have arrived at their views. Hear the stories of others, as we share our own.
6. Exercise care that expressions of personal offense at the differing opinions of others not be used as a means of inhibiting dialogue.
7. Be a patient listener before formulating responses.
8. Be open to change in your own position and patient with the process of change in the thinking and behavior of others.
9. Make use of facilitators and mediators where communication can be served by it.
10. Always remember that people are defined, ultimately, by their relationship with

God—not by the flaws we discover or think
we discover in their views and
actions.(from the Dialogue on Theological
Diversity within the UMC.)

If we were to follow these, hold each other accountable to these, as we confer one with another, we would
do well.

STEP 3: PATIENCE

Some of the above recommendations indicate that
we are to be patient with one another, but I think even
more important for real conferencing is the patience
required to wait on the Holy Spirit. Those whom Wesley
gathered in conference believed that the Spirit of God
was there, in the midst of them, in the midst of their conferring, to guide this emerging Para church preaching
order.

A question in *The Large Minutes* shows the centrality
of seeking the Holy Spirit.

Q. How may we best improve the time of this
Conference?

A. 1. While we are Conversing, let us have an
especial care to set God always before us. 2.
In the intermediate hours, let us redeem all
the time we can for private exercises. 3.
Therein let us give ourselves to prayer for
one another, and for a blessing on this our
labour. (*Works* [Jackson] vol. 8, p. 299.)

Those who met in conference were not there to propose and vote on legislation as though the church were a democracy. *This was not necessarily an efficient process.* They were there to seek the direction of the crucified King with regard to his mission to manifest his reign and redeem fallen creation.

STEP 4: BEARING WITH ONE ANOTHER IN LOVE

In the Preface to his *Sermons on Several Occasions,* which are part of the doctrinal standards for United Methodists, Wesley wrote:

> Are you persuaded you see more clearly than me? It is not unlikely that you may. Then treat me as you would desire to be treated yourself upon a change of circumstances. Point me out a better way than I have yet known. Show me it is so by plain proof of Scripture. And if I linger in the path I have been accustomed to tread and therefore am unwilling to leave it, labor with me a little; take me by the hand and lead me as I am able to bear. ("Preface," *Works,* [Outler], vol. 1.)

All is lost in conferencing if we do not remember to keep love as the goal.

In Wesley's sermon on "The Way to the Kingdom," he asserts that Christianity does not consist of "outward action" or even "orthodoxy or right opinions." A person "May be orthodox on every point. He may not only espouse right opinions, but zealously defend them against all opposers." Yet he may be a stranger to the "Religion of the Heart."

That is not to say that doctrine is unimportant. We must maintain unity in the essentials. However, the mark of a Christian is a heart transformed by the love of God in Christ, to love God and neighbor.

True conferencing provides a forum for us to grow, as a body, in love (which is the chief mark of holiness) that we might manifest the kingdom of God to a confused, alienated, broken, and sick world. This is more important than getting the right answer in a timely fashion.

That means we are, at all cost, to avoid provoking one another to wrath. In the above-mentioned "Preface." Wesley also wrote to those who disagreed with him:

> Perhaps if you are angry, so shall I be too; and then there will be small hopes of finding the truth. If once anger arise . . . this smoke will so dim the eyes of my soul that I shall be able to see nothing clearly. For God's sake, if it be possible to avoid it, let us not provoke one another to wrath. Let us not kindle in each other this fire of hell, much less blow it into flame. ("Preface," *Works*, [Outler], vol. 1.)

Wesley concluded the "Preface" with these words:

> If through anger we cease to love our brother or sister, all is lost. . . . For how far is love, even with many wrong opinions, to be preferred before truth itself without love? We may die without the knowledge of many truths and yet be carried into Abraham's bosom. But if we die without love, what will knowledge avail? ("Preface," *Works*, [Outler], vol. 1.)

God forbid that our conferring should become a stumbling block to salvation. If we allow our differences to result in "anger and resentment" as Wesley wrote in his sermon "On Schism," such tempers "may issue in bitterness, malice, and settled hatred; creating a present hell . . . as a prelude to hell eternal." ("On Schism," *Works*, [Outler], vol. 3.)

If conferring produces evil tempers, conferring should be given up for a time. It has ceased to be a means of grace for its participants. But there is never a time we give up on each other, and certainly not on God.

Conclusion: The Unity of the Spirit in the Bond of Peace

In 1776, an American lay preacher named William Waters wrote this about an annual conference:

> We were of one heart and mind, and took sweet counsel together, not how we should get riches or honors, or anything that this poor world could afford us; but how we should make the surest work for heaven, and be the instruments of saving others. (William Watters, *A Short Account of the Christian Experience and Ministereal Labours of William Watters*, Alexandria: S Snowdon, 1806. Reprinted in *Virginia United Methodist Heritage*, vol. 26 no. 2 [Fall 2000] p. 29.)

When was the last time someone echoed Waters comments about one or our annual conferences?

I fear that, at present, our so-called conferences are so conformed to this world that real conferencing is nearly impossible. We have allowed ourselves to be misguided into the well-worn grooves of the world's Red and Blue politics.

Rather than an encounter with the radical inbreaking of the kingdom of God, we come to conference and encounter a legislature—complete with electronic voting.

The dominant tools taken up here are not humility, gentleness, patience, and bearing with each other in love—not the way of Christ—but subtle coercion and manipulation, gossip and backbiting—the way of the devil.

It might amaze people to find out that at one time conference was a place of expectation—where revival might break out—where people might get converted to God. Conference was a place where tired, worn-out, cynical preachers like me might again catch a glimpse of the reign of God. Conference was where those playing a game of religion could encounter true love. Conference was a place where ordinary people might find something extraordinary to pledge their lives to—a movement of God's Spirit sweeping this world.

As conference now exists in Methodism, it is a perilous endeavor. Many a newcomer may get converted at annual conference, but I fear it is generally not to Jesus.

What if our presence in the cities where we meet to conference were a means of grace to those cities? What if

God's feast could be tasted while we were there? What if God's presence could be brushed up against? What if God's peaceable kingdom was anticipated among us?

Are we trapped in a system of so-called conferencing dominated by the principalities and powers, only fit to be destroyed by fire? Must we persist in this unrighteousness?

Jesus is calling to us Methodists, ". . . the kingdom of God has come near; repent and believe in the good news." (Mk 1:15.)

*Repent*ance is the beginning of Christianity, the doorway to the reign of God, and perhaps the beginning of a renewed practice of conferencing.

This will involve a deep knowing that we have not got it all together—that the system is broken—and that we don't know how to fix it. This will involve placing ourselves in the light of Truth, admitting our pettiness and corruption, our scheming and conniving, our mistreatment of our brother and sister, and our lack of love, and knowing ourselves condemned by that Truth.

Then we need to *believe* in the present existence of the kingdom of God. As Methodists we profess doctrinally that God goes before us, everywhere. There is nowhere that Christ is not. That means that Jesus is here—perhaps abused and mocked by our usurpation and abuse of worldly power—but he is here nonetheless.

And he is a sacrifice for our sin. He is love. He is forgiveness. He is new birth. Life.

Democracy will never bring us to the unity of the

Spirit in the bond of peace. We have an opportunity at our annual conferences to engage in a discipline and a means of grace. Might we try to have a real, perhaps first, annual conference with one another? This is counter-cultural—something this world, with its point/counterpoint and talk radio, knows nothing of.

I pray, for our sakes, for Methodism's sake, that we encounter the God who has judged us and redeemed us in Jesus Christ. I pray that our conferences might be reborn, and that they might become just that—an annual or even a general conference one with another—and a means of grace to all who participate in them.

Chapter Six

A Way Forward

I write this last chapter with more reservation than any of the previous ones. A historian's task is to tell stories about a community's past in order to help that community understand who it is in the present. It is not to tell that community how to make the past live in the present. So I am taking off my historian's hat and writing as a part of the community.

I write this chapter as a person who has been in the United Methodist Church as long as I can remember. I was confirmed and (later) converted to Christ in a United Methodist Church. From elementary school to college, to graduate school, in Iowa, Pennsylvania, North Carolina, and New Jersey, I was an active member of some United Methodist congregation. I have pastored in United Methodist congregations. All of my children have been baptized in the United Methodist Church, and I am currently part of a United Methodist congregation in Hyattsville, Maryland where my family has its membership.

Yet I also write as someone who feels like an outsider. That may seem strange from an ordained United Methodist elder who is a professor in one of the thirteen official United Methodist seminaries. Nonetheless, despite how long I have been part of United Methodism and all the advantages it has afforded me, the denomination has always seemed distant. It has never been what I, through my studies, found so intriguing about John Wesley and the Methodist movement. Yet I have to stick with the Methodists. What I find so lacking in American Christianity generally is found in our tradition. There is nowhere else for me to go.

I entitle this chapter "a way forward," because I know it is not "the" way forward. What I am offering here is not the "fix" for what ails us. What I offer are questions to help us get at a diagnosis. I also offer experiments, different treatments, to try, to see what works and what doesn't. This chapter is me dreaming about what might spur the body to recover Methodism within United Methodism.

This chapter is not a "how to," but it is intended to be practical. What I want to do is get communities talking about God's mission and what it means to be Methodist. The previous chapters lay out a challenge and a vision. This chapter will try to lead us through the process of "so what?" Some of these ideas are for small groups within local United Methodist congregations or for whole congregations who are tired of the way things have been done—who want to try something different from what is. I also hope that these ideas will serve as a model for someone who wants to start new Methodist communities within United Methodism. I put them out there in the hopes that they will spark conversation.

A Renewed Understanding of Church

The way the story of Methodism is often told, we began as a movement and then were forced to grapple with what it meant to be a church. This grappling involved "necessary" changes, which produced structures and practices that gradually came to define us. We matured from a movement into a church, with "civic" architecture, organs and choirs, an educated and *de facto*, settled clergy.

What we rarely examine are the assumptions behind that word "church." The plan we were following for "church" was determined, at least subconsciously, by the European State Church tradition. Denominationalism, which emerged out of the American situation of no one dominant national organization, was a compromise that never really questioned the model fundamentally. What Methodism became in America (and in England after Wesley's death) was an institution whose structure mimicked the way church had been done since "Constantine the Great called himself a Christian," as Wesley himself put it.

> I say "called himself a Christian"; for I dare not
> affirm that *he was one.* . . . for surely there never was
> a time wherein Satan gained so fatal an advantage
> over the church of Christ as when such a flood of
> riches, and honour, and power broke in upon it,
> particularly the clergy." ("Signs of the Times,"
> *Works*, [Jackson], vol. 2.)

An alternative telling of our same history is that
Methodism was always most church, (defined, as Wesley
did, as "a company of faithful" people) when it was a
movement. As it increased in size and popularity,
Constantinian models of what "church" should look like
tempted it. Methodists became more "churchy," and we
gradually ceased to be "one" through schisms, we ceased
to be "holy" through lax discipline and compromise, we
ceased to be "catholic" through denominational preju-
dice, and we ceased to be "apostolic" (that is, a "sent
people") through sloth. When it was finally clear that
Methodism had stopped being a movement, we had
effectively stopped bearing the marks of the Church. We
had become the "dead sect" Wesley feared we would—
nearly as dead as the Constantinian State Church of
England we had been formed to revive.

And yet, in the last fifty years, Christianity has spread
like a virus around the globe. It has mutated in different
environments and host cultures. It has developed ways
of worshipping and organizational structures of dizzying
variety. The Church is alive, and the Church is out of the

control of any one incarnation of it. No longer can European models, however old, claim a monopoly on the definition of "Church." No longer can we assume that churches will eventually conform to the patterns of the great historic churches. This may be scary for some. I find it exciting. The only hope we have is that the Holy Spirit is at work.

The ecumenical conversation today needs to look much different from what it looked like even fifty years ago. In a very messy global church, there is opportunity for Methodists to become a people again—to reclaim our peculiarity as Methodists for the sake of the larger Church, and not simply mimic the established patterns of "Church."

This could mean (as it once did) that one could be Methodist and be part of any local church of whatever denomination. It certainly means that being part of a United Methodist congregation doesn't make you a Methodist. It may also mean relocating to the margins of society, where we began, and allowing the gospel to do what the gospel does, trickle up.

Methodist societies were intended to bear witness to honest Christian society where ordinary people could encounter it. My suspicion is that the recovery of Methodism will be easiest for those who already realize they are "marginal"—churches that are smaller, or rural, or inner city, or working class, or new starts, or not European American. It may start with groups of individuals in churches starting class meetings on their own.

- Is our faith community's identity primarily mainline or Methodist?
- What does "success" look like for our community?
- What would look different if we self-consciously chose to be Methodist?

A Renewed Vision

When I say we need a renewed vision, I am not advocating that we come up with a new "vision statement." Every local church, it seems, is trying to construct a vision statement as though each community were independent and could have its own vision. I'll grant that a local church defining a vision is better than having no vision beyond its own institutional continuation. However, what makes us "the people called Methodists" is that we do not get to determine the vision. We don't have that prerogative. To be Methodist is to become part of a vision that has captured us and is bigger than our local churches, our conferences, our country, and our century.

Every action taken in any Methodist community should flow from a vision of what God has done, is doing, and will do at the end of time. This is not a vision of large, full sanctuaries, of overflowing youth groups, and Sunday schools. This is a vision of God's will being done on earth as in heaven, in the lives of people seeking to be faithful, and in their social interactions in the world. This is a vision of reform, of "spreading scriptural holiness."

The General Conference of the United Methodist Church has come up with an official vision statement: "to make disciples of Jesus Christ for the transformation of the world." While there is nothing wrong with the first part of this statement (it comes from the Great Commission) there is also nothing Methodist about it. Any Christian could say it. It is another attempt to pretend we are the whole church, not a peculiar order within the Church.

I do not find the current "vision" for the United Methodist Church to be an improvement on our given vision of reforming "the continent by spreading scriptural holiness over these lands." Committing to our historic vision has the potential to bring actual change, abandoning the standards of success (size, wealth, popularity, power) by which we have been measuring ourselves for generations. The language of "scriptural holiness" will also change the categories for our disagreements. It clarifies whose version of a transformed world we are aiming at.

We United Methodists have been playing church for a long time without being a Christian society. We have been "having a form of godliness, but denying the power thereof." (2 Timothy 3:5, KJV.) Our focus on big yields has ended up polluting the very soil we are expected to till. As long as we seek first the world, we are not offering salvation to the world, and the disciples we make will not be equipped to follow the Master.

- What is our church's vision?
- How is that vision related to God's final purpose—a holy creation in harmony with His will?
- Does our church consciously seek to spread scriptural holiness? How?

A Renewed Commitment to Salvation

A renewed commitment to holiness necessitates a renewed commitment to salvation, since holiness is the purpose of salvation. I have been privileged to be part of groups that are actively seeking holiness together. We haven't quite gotten there yet, but we are striving. We don't make excuses for the lack of full salvation in ourselves and the world around us. Nothing that opposes the will of God, nothing that holds us or anyone else in bondage to sin is "okay."

Such a renewed commitment to salvation means repentance and faith over and over again. "There is also a repentance and a faith," Wesley wrote,

> which are requisite after we have "believed the gospel;" yea, and in every subsequent stage of our Christian course, or we cannot "run the race which is set before us." And this repentance and faith are full as necessary, in order to our continuance and growth in grace, as the former faith and repentance were, in order to our entering into the kingdom of

God." ("Repentence of Believers" *Works,* [Jackson],
vol. 5.)

The truth is most of us who are believers are not running that race very well. The blood of Jesus was poured
out to *remove* our unfaithfulness and we have made the
blood of Jesus a *covering* for our unfaithfulness.

I remember when the BTK serial killer was captured
in Kansas and it was revealed that he was, not just a
member, but also a leader in his local church. I remember breathing a sigh of relief that at least he wasn't a
Methodist. But I knew that he could have been. There is
nothing in our current structure that brings people face
to face with the expectations of a Christ-shaped life. And
nothing that brings them into the kind of relationships
with each other over spiritual matters that could have
put the breaks on that man's slide into his own depravity and the demonic terror that slide unleashed.

Methodism not only found ways to connect with the
Holy Spirit, but it insisted people cooperate with the
Holy Spirit by making use of instituted and prudential
means of grace. As it says in Psalm 34:14 (often quoted
by John Wesley), Methodism existed to help people
"depart from evil and do good."

To do this again, we need to readopt the General
Rules as the basis for membership. We can reclaim our
identity as an order with a rule of life within the larger
Church. An order within the larger church has a particular way of ordering their life together. The rules are

helps—means of grace—to aid in serving God. They detail the expectations the community has for one another and the structures they submit to. The General Rules determine who is and who is not a Methodist. Therefore, Methodism must allow and insist people to leave the order when they no longer wish to live into them. Leaving does not mean a person is leaving the Church, just the order.

In this new era of ecumenism, Methodism needs to realize that we are not the Church; we are a way of being Christian within the Church. This means not everybody has to be one of us. Methodism is not about worldly numbers and power; it is about providing living witnesses to the new creation.

To be Methodist is not to disparage the larger Church. Methodism at its best is a lay order of the Church. Methodism is not a church (whatever that means). We baptize, and we celebrate the Eucharist as a part of the one, holy, catholic, and apostolic body. But receiving the rites of the whole Church from Methodist hands does not make one a Methodist anymore than receiving the sacraments at a Roman Catholic church run by the Franciscans makes one a monk.

The General rules do not mean that those who follow them are better Christians than those who do not. These rules do not even mean one is a Christian, at least not as Wesley would define it. The Methodist order expects that a person will begin to submit to the rule of life *before* he or she becomes a real Christian. Real

Christianity will happen in God's time by the working of the Holy Spirit, who witnesses "with our spirit that we are children of God." (Rm 8:18.) In essence, Wesley was restoring the catechumenate, with the experience of justification replacing baptism for those who had been baptized as infants.

- How does our community take seriously a commitment to Wesleyan notions of grace?
- How do we actively place ourselves in God's grace?
- Where are the people who are struggling under the weight of sin and sinful structures?
- How are we introducing them to "Christ in all his offices?"

A Renewed Method

If we are going to be serious about cooperating with grace to make saints, instead of cooperating with the world to build big impressive institutions, we need to find ways (some of which will be humiliating) to methodically cooperate with the Holy Spirit. If United Methodism is to mean anything, beyond generic Protestantism "with some peculiar opinions and modes of worship" then we must find places to restore the discipline that once defined our corporate life.

That means aggressively confronting the world with

the reality of sin and inviting the world that God "so loved" into the kingdom of forgiveness and new life. Now, whenever anyone mentions something like field preaching, most United Methodists flee. We say we want to work for justice and redemption, but we are so polite to all that opposes God. We don't want to turn anyone off.

One of my students, who is gifted in visual art, created a DVD. The images on the DVD were local, recognizable, and accessible. They were set to music with a message appearing throughout as text that expressed God's love for all and God's desire that people return to God. The student's plan was to pass them out in front of the coffee shop at the same time everyday for a week and then hang out in the coffee shop. Those who took a copy of the DVD would see him again and be intrigued. He would be there to engage anyone who wished in a discussion about the gospel and invite them to something deeper, to a bible study or church.

This may not be a submission to vileness as dramatic as Wesley's, but it does put us out there, in the public conversation, vulnerable. I admit I don't know exactly what preaching at the market cross looks like today. I suspect it doesn't look all that different from what it looked like in the eighteenth century. In any case, whatever it looks like, we will not be able to do it and maintain our detached respectability.

Restoring our corporate discipline also means establishing small groups that meet weekly for fellowship, perhaps some worship and study, but most importantly to ask each other, "How does your soul prosper" or, to translate, "How are you doing spiritually?"

Class meetings are the standard for Methodist membership. Admittedly, it has been a long time since we even thought about such a thing as a denomination. When Methodism finally removed the requirement for class meetings in 1939 at the Union of the Northern and Southern branches of the church with the Methodist Protestants, it was simply the acknowledgement of a fact of church life that began in the late nineteenth century. Membership and class meeting attendance were not related. For true Methodism to revive, they need to become reacquainted.

One hope of mine is that normal churchgoers seeing the low level of spiritual expectation and community in many United Methodist Churches will decide to form classes on their own. Apart from the rules of membership and checking in weekly there is nothing complicated about such meetings, and one certainly doesn't need anyone's permission.

If anyone is beginning a new Christian society (a.k.a. a church plant) based on the principles of Methodism, I would suggest beginning with class structure. Just have a simple organization: a local elder whose responsibility is to Word, Sacrament, and Order for the local congregation, and class leaders who are responsible for the spiritual and physical well being of the members of the class, and thus of the society. All other ministry structures, in which non-members would be encouraged to participate, should be left to the community to figure out.

If anyone currently serving a congregation wanted to move toward a class structure, one could begin with new members, and grandfather in all the current members (who came in under the old system). For the current members who want to be part of the change, adult Sunday school classes could easily be modified to incorporate class meeting "checking in."

Of course, accountability is not just for the lay people. It must also be for the leadership, and at a higher level. All leaders, class leaders and elders, should be expected to be earnestly seeking the vision of Methodism, seeking holiness. They should be expected to be part of a band meeting, practicing the discipline of confession, "confessing sins one to another that they might be healed." (James 5:16.)

The great thing about itinerancy was that it provided another level of accountability, of apostolic oversight. An apostle is one who is "sent" (the meaning of the Greek word *apostello*) from place to place to establish new communities and hold older communities of faith accountable to the structured discipline of the Church. Just as "superintendent" was a translation of the meaning of the Greek word for bishop (*episcopos*), itinerant captured this meaning of apostolic. Like Paul did on his travels, the itinerancy provided someone from the outside who would visit, correct, and exhort a local society.

United Methodism needs to acknowledge that itinerancy does not really exist. As soon as churches grew big enough and rich enough to "employ" a stationed pastor, the itinerancy began to disappear. When Elders wanted to remain in ministry with families and steady income and congregations wanted ministers who were always present, it began to fall apart. As elders became present, the role of local preacher and class leader diminished and the ability of the elder to have a real prophetic ministry did as well.

The problem with no itinerancy is that there is no real outside accountability. Clergy and laity alike can easily seek a comfortable coexistence without accountability. We as pastors are too close to our communities and too dependent on them to really discipline them or to have them discipline us.

What would it look like if those communities who were committed to being Methodist within the United Methodist structure, classes within larger congregations, new church starts, or established churches who want a change, recruited traveling accountability partners who would visit our congregations bi-yearly or yearly to see if we are actually adhering to the standards of Methodism?

This would mean that elders in local congregations would have to give up power. The itinerant accountability partners would have the authority to enforce the rules and structure of the societies. Itinerants would have the authority to put a church or class on probation or even acknowledge that they are no longer *de facto* part of the connection of communities experimenting with Methodism within the larger United Methodist connection.

- What would it mean to give up all the structures of the local Methodist church except those that methodically cooperate with God's grace at every stage?
- What has to remain and why?
- What would it look like to reinstitute something equivalent to field preaching, classes and bands? Could it be done today?

A Renewed Conversation

What structures can put us in real conversation with each other instead of lobbing bombs at each other from entrenched positions? Can we give up Robert's Rules of Order? Can we give up democracy?

For those communities that would like to pursue Methodism, I would suggest a yearly meeting of leaders who would like to attend. This conference would be different from the annual conferences. First, each meeting would be small enough to have a conversation.

At this conference we could actually confer about the main questions that Methodism asked. "What to teach?" "How to teach?" "What to do?" always with the main vision of perfection and spreading scriptural holiness before the group. Questions can be submitted from any of the participating class meetings, societies. They should be questions, which need an answer for the continuing of ministry in our various settings. *Questions. Discussion. Consensus. No legislation.*

If needed, a moderator or overseer for this conversation could be chosen by lot. The moderator's job would be to determine the consensus of the community. If no consensus can be reached on a given question, then we wait to speak until there is consensus.

Choosing leaders by lot is, after all, part of our heritage. Matthias was added to the Twelve by lot; John Wesley was persuaded to begin preaching in Bristol through a kind of casting of lots. Martin Boehm was made elder and then bishop by the casting of lots. The word for clergy comes from the Greek word, *kleros*, or lot. It would be a good discipline for us Methodists to give up our commitment to democracy.

This would involve a step in faith beyond most Methodists, which is precisely what we need to start doing. I have often heard it said that it is an act of faith to believe God works through the process we have now, usually from people who have a vested interest in the process. I wonder what it would take for us to believe that the Holy Spirit is capable of working when we give up our imagined power and control through the process. By casting lots we would force ourselves to believe that the Holy Spirit can work without our systems.

- Where and when could we gather in small enough groups to discuss the issues that impede us from doing mission?
- Where do we ask the three questions about what to teach, how to teach, and what to do?

Conclusion

Methodism began as a means of grace and a system of accountability. It was an order within the larger church for the renewal of the Church. If we are to recover that usefulness to the kingdom of God in the world, we need what we once had: a missional focus, clear simple rules, and a clear simple and flexible structure.

All of this could be done within the structure of the current United Methodist Church. But it will not be universally appreciated. I am sure that such a reordering of the corporate life of some United Methodist churches and small groups will be costly. Discipleship always is. Recovery from an illness is rarely fun or easy. But it is better than the alternative, which is not recovering.

My hope is that these chapters have provided the beginnings of a thoughtful conversation about what it means to be Methodist and perhaps a beginning for renewal. I long to see the day when Methodism will once again be a visible, if numerically smaller, presence on the spiritual landscape. I long for companies of the faithful to be once more living and dying for the spread of scriptural holiness across these lands.